WILDERNESS
CANOEING

Also by John W. Malo

MALO'S COMPLETE GUIDE
TO CANOEING AND CANOE-CAMPING

CANOEING

John W. Malo

WILDERNESS
CANOEING

The Macmillan Company, New York, New York
Collier-Macmillan Ltd., London

To Doctors Harold Emiley and Robert Kuehnert,

     who shared the baptism in wilderness canoeing,

     happy wanderings on blue waters,

     under the Northern Lights,

     where for each hundred miles traveled,

     there are a thousand memories.

ACKNOWLEDGMENTS

My grateful thanks to . . .

Members of the staffs of the Canadian Government Travel Bureau,

The departments, bureaus, divisions, and agencies of the various provinces of Canada,

The officials of the departments, bureaus, divisions, and agencies of the United States Government and members of their staffs,

The officials of the departments and bureaus of the various states and their staffs . . .

Who have furnished information and encouragement in the writing of this book;

Ralph Frese, canoe manufacturer, conservationist, and Modern Voyageur, and

"Uncle" Don Johnson of Farm and Wilderness Camps, Vermont, for their counsel and support;

The Outdoor Writers Association of America for judging my previous books worthy of citation for "contributing to the awareness of the recreational potential of the nation's waterways and the need for preservation of the natural beauty of these waters";

Adele M. Ries, consultant, who exhibits the virtues of the wilderness canoeist—fortitude, determination, and cooperation.

✺ Contents

✿ Foreword

THE basic lures of wilderness canoeing lie within the clean country with a far horizon, a vast sky, and the nearness of the stars at night—providing an opportunity to think clearly, to plumb the depths of one's self, to find solace in unfathomable solitude.

To the adventurous soul, wilderness canoeing offers an opportunity to wander and to wonder, to find his place in the physical universe as, disdaining the soft life with its stresses of daily living in an unnatural environment, in complete separation from familiar surroundings, he enjoys the immediate values of purposeful exercise, pitting his strength against the odds of a series of tasks in a natural environment.

The wilderness canoeist travels long distances; he predetermines his route, sometimes to retrace some water trail traveled by historic figures; he prepares for his trip; and then he proceeds to fulfill his aim, to achieve his goal, and is rewarded by turbulent waters, by scenic wonders, and by the deep satisfactions of accomplishing his objectives.

The wind and the rain may come up to lash his body and his craft, but he will paddle furiously and, upon reaching his destination, look back at his achievement with the exhilarating thrill of conquest, the glow of success. Then his rewards compound: the sun reappears, the roar of water abates, the fragrance of resinous pines pervades the air; he takes a refreshing drink of cool water, pitches camp, and cooks his meal.

At night he climbs a high point of land, lies on his back and watches the heavens. In addition to the stars and the constellations, never more vivid, he probably witnesses the grand display of the aurora borealis (Northern Lights), and stays up till dawn admiring heaven's most awe-inspiring phenomena— the wavering and the flickering, the rising and the falling of celestial patterns in rose-red, pale green, magenta, and purplish cold flares. In northern climes, the lights cover the entire sky, from horizon to horizon. He gains insights into the grand plan of the universe, and they humble him.

Regardless of the miles the veteran canoeist has behind him, on each trip he assuredly can anticipate the unusual, the learning of something new as he solves the unique problems with original solutions and techniques— even the experiencing of new joys.

The suggestions and directions in this book have not only come from one man's experience with many groups of various ages and of both sexes, under wilderness conditions, but also have been checked with others, and are offered in the hope of enhancing your experiences and contributing to your safety in the wilderness, for canoe-camping offers life-long recreational enjoyment, it being one of the "carry-over sports" that can be engaged in and enjoyed for many years, without requiring brute strength, exacting skills, or an intense spirit of competition.

xi

Part One

❧ ❧ ❧

BEFORE THE PADDLE
IS WETTED

❧ ❧ ❧

1

The Adventuring Man

THERE'S a resurgence of interest in wild places, and the canoe can penetrate water-woods wildernesses farther and more effectively than the automobile, the horse, or hiking shoes.

Leaving at home the pampering comforts and the artificial mechanical advantages of civilized living, men and women of all ages are paddling canoes on quiet waters in spirit-lifting solitude, in rhythmic movement are cruising wave-lapped, pine-crowned, granite-rimmed lakes, are pitting their wits and their strength against the white waters of roaring rivers, relishing meals of their own cooking around campfires, and at remote campsites are sleeping peacefully under the big sky.

In pairs, in threes, in family groups, and in larger circles of enthusiasts paddling flotillas, moderns in ever-increasing numbers are finding adventure in the efficient, hand-propelled craft that was invented by primitive man and evolved and adapted by the Indians to provide sure and secure transportation necessary for survival—to take them fishing and hunting, to move their families and their household goods as weather, seasonal changes, and food sources required.

Since the latter part of the nineteenth century in our country, the canoe has been a recreational watercraft without peer: today, its popularity stems from a romantic past, and it continues to be the most logical craft for adventure. The efficient canoe of inherited design draws little water, requires but a few inches for flotation, performs with stability in high winds and in turbulent waters, and with little effort moves in a straight line.

The modern canoe is light in weight, easy to transport to water, just as easy to portage across land, and is available in aluminum, fiber glass, or wood-canvas, in sizes and models to suit any purpose—from overnight

trips to months away from base camp ground. To enjoy the sport, there are numerous agencies and outfitters across the land that rent not only canoes but also camping equipment and gear and also furnish grub.

Twentieth-century recreationists are pushing farther out from concentrations of population for that confrontation with nature that earlier generations of natives, of explorers, pioneers, missionaries, and the hardy early settlers knew.

On the water and in the woods, beyond the gray concrete, in backwoods areas whose primitive, primeval character remains as it existed hundreds of years ago, modern adventurous canoe-campers are finding respite from harsh elements inherent in urban and suburban living.

Wilderness canoeing satisfies the deep-rooted yearning for a change of pace in unspoiled, wild places, fulfills the wish to strip life down to its essentials. The adventure begins where the hard pavement ends and the car is parked, where the canoeists, their craft, equipment, and gear are dropped off on a Canadian railroad siding, or where a pilot of a bush plane touches down on a remote stretch of water. At that moment, their ties with civilization are severed, freeing the crew of compatible canoeists to experience the independence of all the adventurous generations who have preceded them, and to grapple with the truth of their own self-reliance.

At their embarkation point, the crew points the bow of their canoe and weaves farther and farther along silvery water trails into the hinterland to enjoy otherwise inaccessible scenic wonders, new-found fishing holes, remote geographical and historical sites, and the glow of discovering one's inner resources.

The wilderness experience provides an opportunity for canoeists to learn cooperative living in an entirely new dimension. In the urban structure of our lives, food, shelter, and clothing are not necessarily self-provided, but are bought, rented, or bestowed. In wilderness living, each member of a group has to relate to the others: he has duties to perform and roles to fulfill which are neither abstractions nor merely ideological—the real situations are there, neither invented nor contrived. The tasks must be completed, for cooperation has a survival basis, being both cause and effect. If any crew member fails to

meet his obligation, the group simply does not eat adequately, sleep properly, have time for fishing, prospecting, or other hobbies, or for negotiating the planned route.

Inherent in a wilderness trip are opportunities to learn the responsibilities of a pioneering nature whereby the group, on its own, establishes a form of self-government, which not only brings responsibility into focus, but also gives experiences in democratic control. Each group of wilderness trippers establishes the rules under which they will operate, and having done this, crew members are inclined to follow through on them. A new concept of freedom is achieved—not the "do as I please" freedom, but liberty on a higher and more effective plane.

They who seek the adventures afforded by canoe travel on the waterways of this con-

". . . continues to be the most logical craft for adventure."
PROVINCE OF QUEBEC FILM BUREAU PHOTO

"... recreationists are pushing farther out ... for that confrontation with nature."

SASKATCHEWAN GOVERNMENT PHOTO

At Jungfrau Lake, Ontario, canoeists have been dropped off, and the bush plane, their last contact with civilization, takes off.

ONTARIO DEPT. TOURISM & INFORMATION PHOTO

tinent are greatly rewarded in the exercising of their ingenuity, in the overcoming of obstacles, and in the development of creative activities, for never are two extended canoe-camping trips alike; the unanticipated, the unusual, crops up every time, and sometimes the contributions of the neophyte proves to be invaluable.

Almost anyone can enjoy a wilderness experience once he knows the basics of canoeing and camping. Brute strength is not a necessary ingredient of the skills of canoeing, for many diminutive girls and women are as skillful as are men in paddling great distances, in handling the light craft on land, and in general campcraft.

In her book, *Down a Wild River North*, Constance Helmericks relates an interesting wilderness canoe trip through one of the last great wildernesses in North America, Canada's Northwest Territory.

Confronted, like many modern-day mothers, with two teen-age daughters—fond of boys, comfortable, and saucy—she decided to give them a rugged experience. They set out in a twenty-foot freighter canoe to follow the route of great explorers on the Peace, Slave, Mackenzie, and Red rivers, the greatest river system in Canada—a vast chain of rivers and lakes, of rapids and swamps—whose torturous course rambles northwestward from the middle of Alberta to the Arctic Coast, just east of Alaska.

The all-female crew, in canoeing the watershed, learned its importance to the land—a country much cleaner and more beautiful than anything they had ever seen—met Indians and Eskimos along the way, experienced the forces of nature, and came to grips with elements that are bigger and older than the society that had bred them.

On our second trip into the Ontario wilderness above the fifty-second parallel, the author prevailed upon Doctors Harold Emiley

Entering the Basswood River, Minnesota-Canada Boundary waters, for an extended canoe trip.
COURTESY COLORADO SPORTS CORP.

and Robert Kuehnert to include some young, inner-city, high school men in the crew, one of whom was a natural leader, sophisticated in the ways of the street-corner "gang." Upon plunging into the nowhere of the alien domain of the wilds—where bluff and status are useless—realizing that the problems were outside his experience, our friend became frightened with frustration and introverted.

The wilderness wove her magic spell. In the company of other members of the crew who relished every aspect of the required regimen, long before the trip was over, our protégé, forgetting the "muscle" fostered by money, became a cheerful contributing hand, and enjoyed every phase of wilderness canoe-camping.

Each one who has a little Daniel Boone in his soul and is able should answer the call of the wilderness, and with at least one companion, with the water and the big sky as the backdrop of your domain, you'll meet life on its most simple terms. As the wilderness trip unfolds, mile after mile, day after day, you'll come to know the taste of perspiration on your lips, the heat of the sun on your back, the fatigue of a day's paddle, the benediction of a campfire after a purposeful day, and the deep sleep to renew the forces for the morrow.

When the cold night descends, you're prepared for it as you are for the rain and the wind, the bugs and the hunger. True, for some, especially those who live softly, overeat, and under-exercise, at first it may be difficult to face up, but in time each learns to deal with his own mind and muscle and to resolve those things that have to be done. The attitudes of overcoming adversity will develop, and they will keep a canoeist in good stead for the rest of his life.

Wilderness areas, "far from the madding crowd," preserve their primeval character by their very ruggedness and inaccessibility. The backwoods land and water are free of the many forces that work to destroy natural realms. Absent are the extensive solitude-destroying ventures of man. In the United States and Canada there are unspoiled wildernesses remaining in a state of grace that have so far survived the population explosion to remain clean and serene, wild and free—free of soft drink bottles, of beer cans, and of chewing gum wrappers.

In this day of spreading population, most of the wild rivers and the remote lakes are in Alaska, northern Canada, and parts of Maine, Pennsylvania, Florida, Michigan, Minnesota, and Wisconsin: however, a wilderness canoe-camping experience also is possible in nearby waters, for wind and rain, hail, and rushing water can, and do, produce conditions to set back the calendar as if some mad scientist's fictional time clock had gone

Drying out gear after being caught on a lake during a rainstorm.
HAROLD EMILEY PHOTO, USED BY PERMISSION

awry, had stripped away civilization, and challenge the canoeist with all the problems faced by the Indians before the white man came upon the scene. This can be as true of a river near your home as it is of certain shores of the Great Lakes, the Mississippi, Missouri, Okefenokee, Columbia, Colorado, Hudson, and the Ohio rivers and their tributaries, to name a few.

Not all the canoeing frontiers lie halfway around the world: some are within reach of many stateside cities. Wilderness waters are where you find them.

The canoe can meander along waterways incapable of carrying larger craft, and during the trip the canoeists find a true wilderness aspect and challenge—regardless of their geographical proximity to population density.

The inexpressible romance of eighteen feet of craft carrying passengers and all the necessities of life to a natural environment is perhaps modern man's need, the answer to many of his problems. Man is a part of nature, and in wilderness canoeing he identifies with her in an active way, comes to know her—and himself. After all, this haunting urge has been steadfast for thousands of years, and if it shows signs of diminishing, man is diminished.

Take your canoe onto the distant and unchanged trails of history, traveled first by the native red man, then by the lusty Voyageurs, and with them, the missionaries and the earliest white settlers. Paddle ancient waters and view rocks bearing pictures drawn by early wilderness inhabitants, battle the strong currents and the winds, portage around rapids, curse or praise the changing weather, sing by the campfire—as canoeists throughout the centuries have done. You will gain insights into the freedom of the Indian, the courage of the Voyageurs, and the sacrifice of the missionaries. The chances are that you will emulate these virtues.

The canoe can meander along watery trails where other craft can't enter. Two canoeists enjoy the Waupeca Chain.
WISCONSIN NATURAL RESOURCES DEPT. PHOTO

REFERENCES

To get the most out of any canoe trip, place yourself in the perspective of all who have gone before and used the canoe as their mode of transportation through the vast wildernesses. There are many books dealing with the history and the lore of canoeing and canoeists—the Voyageurs, the fur-trade competition, the contributions of the missionaries and pioneers. Become acquainted with the role of the Hudson's Bay Company, the North West Company, and various historic personalities who traveled in canoes. That background will aid in deepening your appreciation, in giving real meaning as well as added zest to your canoe trips.

Here are but a few of the excellent books available:

The North West Company, by M. W. Campbell (St. Martin's Press, Inc., New York, 1957), includes a list of early explorers' and fur-traders' journals.

The Voyageur's Highway, by Grace Lee Nute (Minnesota Historical Society, St. Paul, Minn., 1941).

Canoe Trails through Quetico, by Keith Denis (Quetico Foundations Publications, University of Toronto Press, Toronto, Canada, 1959).

The Singing Wilderness (1956), *Listening Point* (1958), *The Lonely Land* (1961), *Runes of the North* (1963), by Siguard F. Olson (A. A. Knopf, Inc., New York).

Portage into the Past, by Arnold J. Bolz (University of Minnesota Press, St. Paul, Minn., 1960).

Canoeing with the Cree, by Eric Sevareid (Minnesota Historical Society, St. Paul, Minn., 1968).

Canoe Routes of the Voyageurs, by Eric W. Morse (Minnesota Historical Society, St. Paul, Minn., 1962).

✸ 2 ✸

Planning
the Wilderness
Trip

PROPER planning contributes to an assurance of comfort and safety on a canoe-camping trip in the solitude of the wilderness. Carrying with them all of their needs for survival—canoe, shelter, food, utensils, tools, first-aid supplies, sleeping and personal gear, as well as a load of exuberance—the crew is confidently self-assured.

No modern canoeist need enter the wilderness clothed in fringed buckskins, transporting jerked meat, pemmican, parched corn, a tightly rolled blanket, and a flintlock rifle, as did those in whose footsteps and water trails he follows. Add to the technological advances in fabric manufacture used in modern tentage, clothing, and sleeping bags the development of concentrated, dehydrated, and freeze-dried foods, and you have a boon to present-day canoeists. Subtract the risks of an unknown land which were the lot of our predecessors, and you have the privileges of experiencing

a pure and free portion of the land, a true taste of wild places.

Any canoeist intending to be a member of a crew going on a wilderness canoe-camping trip must be fairly well conditioned physically.* He must have mastered all of the basic canoeing skills, and not gloss over, to himself or others, any inadequacies. A background in outdoor activities—boating, camping, cooking, and swimming—is absolutely essential. A knowledge of simple weather signs is another "must" (see Chapter 8).

Like mountain climbing, whose objective is also to rove beyond the civilized fringes of crowds and concrete, wilderness canoeing is in a sense a team sport and requires discipline.

* Appendix, "A Personal Conditioning Program for Canoeists," *Malo's Complete Guide to Canoeing and Canoe-Camping*, cloth, Quadrangle Books, Inc., Chicago, Illinois, 1969; paperback, New York, Collier Books, 1969.

At all times, each member of the crew must place the welfare of all above his individual ideas, inclinations, and wishes. If one member of the crew is disheartened over some element of the situation, he should be mature, keep his disappointment to himself, and not inflict his negative mood on the others.

Courage and confidence, requisites for members of any team, are especially pertinent to members of a crew. Courage consists of part knowledge, part ability, and part experience. Always, it should be tempered with intelligence. In emergency situations, whether on land or water, courage alone, or brash over-confidence from underestimating the forces of nature, can lead to grief.

In the minds of inexperienced canoeists are two divergent concepts: one, that their mu-

Whether the three in a canoe are of the same generation (A), or three different generations (B), crew members must be compatible. Many friendly combinations enjoy cruising the Lincoln Heritage Trail. ILLINOIS DEPARTMENT OF CONSERVATION PHOTOS

tual interests automatically engender harmony and good feeling among members of the crew; the other, that in the wild, open spaces there is a wide berth for soloing in meditation (abjuring any close ties to fellow crew members) and enjoying an idyllic opportunity to escape from interaction with the others.

In reality, three crew members are close together in a canoe, paddling as a team, portaging canoe and gear along paths; and not too far away from one another at campsites, where frequently the area of level land is small, with limited space for roaming. At night and during inclement weather, crew members huddle together in one or more tents, depending on the size of the party. Such close proximity, day in and day out, is difficult for an over-sensitive person inclined to irritability, who could destroy the morale of the group.

It is important to limit the crew to "compatible friends."

Choose the Proper Canoe

The type of trip being planned determines the kind of canoe for the wilderness experience. Consider the twenty-foot canoe if your route will be confined mainly to large lakes and connecting waters, strong winds, and a minimum number of portages.

For wilderness travel, the eighteen-foot Guide or Prospector canoe is probably the best choice, as it is stable in winds and on rough waters. Because it can be handled more efficiently under a variety of cruising conditions, a keelless model is preferred.

Construction may be of wood-canvas, of aluminum, or of fiber glass.

An outboard clamped to the transom of a square-end canoe on Little Sioux River.
IOWA CONSERVATION COMMISSION PHOTO

Square or Double Ended?

If a square-end canoe, for the accommodation of an outboard motor, is used, to prevent drag or wake, the flat face of the transom should not continue below the water line. In general, square-stern canoes of large size are practical only for freighting heavy cargo on large bodies of water. Generally trappers,

When the outboard motor is to be used on only portions of the wilderness trip, screw a detachable motor bracket at a comfortable arm's distance on the port side of the stern.

EVINRUDE MOTOR DIVISION PHOTO

hunters, prospectors, and other commercial users employ the large canoe-outboard motor combination.

Much better for the recreationist who has but occasional use for a motor is the double-pointed canoe. When the use of an outboard motor is called for, screw a detachable motor bracket to the gunwales at the stern. Anchor the motor to the bracket at a comfortable arm's distance on the port side.

What Size Canoe?

Sixteen-foot canoes and under are impractical for wilderness canoeing.

The seventeen- and eighteen-foot canoes give adequate roominess for cargo and for extra passengers: they have great carrying capacity; are light enough for portaging; and are safe.

In general, the flat-bottomed canoes are more stable than round-bottom models. The straight-keeled, narrow, round-bottom models are for the racing enthusiast.

Keep in mind the important fact that each foot of length adds approximately five pounds to the weight of the canoe and increases its carrying capacity about seventy pounds.

Check up on the Condition of the Canoe

The canoe is the most important piece of equipment in extended tripping. A thorough check-up of its condition is of utmost importance:

    CANVAS-COVERED CANOE: Check for water-soaked planking, cracked ribs, bulges or blisters in the canvas, and for other evidences of deterioration, especially along the gunwales and the keel.

    ALUMINUM CANOE: Check for loose rivets and bolts, and for separations at all overlaps of the aluminum. Also, make

Canoes with their outboards load up at the edge of Lac Brule in the remote Mingan Reserve of virgin lakes in Northern Quebec.
CANADIAN GOVERNMENT TRAVEL BUREAU PHOTO

certain that the flotation chambers are undamaged.

FIBER GLASS CANOE: Look for cracks and separations. Also check for symmetry along the keel line (while inverted) to determine warpage and distortion of stream line.

In all models, check for strong thwarts, decks, firm seats, rope hooks or holes.

The Bush Plane Fly-in

Should a bush plane fly-in be in your plans for the wilderness trip, there is little cause for concern: the advantages are many. The services of a fly-in operator probably assure the best of all available means of reaching remote wildernesses: in fact, without the bush pilot

and his pontooned plane, the most remote hinterland would be unattainable.

The bush pilots are well qualified. Although they do not fly by sophisticated instruments, and are not directed by a control tower or a radio, they fly by their seasoned wits. Their only problem is the weather. Wilderness canoe areas are spotted with hundreds of lakes, and should wind turbulence develop, or any other emergency arise, the float plane can be put down almost anywhere.

Don't hold a pilot too close to the announced schedule, for canoeists, like fishermen, are not always on the top of the list of priorities. We were scheduled to fly out from the Hudson's Bay Post at Deer Lake, Ontario, on a certain day, but as the day ebbed, we were concerned about the arrival of the plane.

"He'll be here," Ian Cruikshank, the post manager, assured us.

Later, the plane appeared, flying in from the north instead of from the south.

"Had to pick up some fish from the Sandy Lake Indians—before they spoiled," the pilot explained. The interior of the plane was stacked to the ceiling with tubs of iced-down whitefish which the Indians had netted.

"But we were supposed to fly out today!" we exclaimed.

"No sweat," the pilot replied as he proceeded to wedge our duffel and gear between the tubs. The lightweight passengers had to sit on the laps of the heavier ones. As the plane taxied over Deer Lake, then raced attempting to gain speed, we thought, "We're running out of lake!" At the last possible moment, barely missing the tops of tall pines, the plane rose. Once airborne, there was "no sweat."

The smaller Cessna planes carry canoes lashed to the under-structure. The large Norsemen and Beechcraft planes carry the canoes inside the craft. Probably due to competition between an increasing number of planes, the service is improving and the flying fees are lower than in former years.

The Services of Outfitters

A decision centering around the services of an outfitter is usually made early in the planning stage. In wilderness-camping areas, there are well-qualified outfitters, natives who know their business in guaranteeing the comfort and the safety of the crew. It is highly recommended that trippers use their counsel and services, for they can fill you in on water conditions, can delineate routes, offer alternate-route choices, indicate the best camping sites, the most promising fishing possibilities and lures, as well as local methods that pay off in a full stringer, etc.

Experienced canoeists who, over the years, have amassed most of the necessities for wilderness travel, use partial outfitting. Should there be any need for last-minute fill-ins, such as an extra ax or paddle, specialized foods, waterproof maps, reflector oven, air mattresses, etc., the outfitter is your last contact for supplies.

You can be completely outfitted for approximately nine dollars per day, per person.

Guides Are Available

Should there be any misgivings about your own ability to make the trip a success, you can hire a guide for the whole trip, or perhaps for one day to enable him to evaluate your equipment, gear, your experience and proposed route, with critical appraisal and suggestions.

Pre-Trip Planning

A spirit of cooperation between trippers is indispensable, even during the frequent pre-trip planning sessions in which every piece of equipment and gear, down to the last safety pin, is challenged, debated, discussed, and agreed on.

A trip leader must emerge and be designated during the planning sessions to assume the responsibility of bringing together all the varied details of the venture, raising such questions as: "Where shall we go?" "How long shall we be gone?" "What are our objectives?" ("What shall we do?" "What shall we see?")

Once the details of starting point, destination, and route have been mutually determined, thorough study should follow:

1. Do a thorough research job of the area to be covered by getting in touch with other people who are familiar with that region. The individual, outfitter, game warden, forest

ranger, Mountie, or park official, to whom all questions should be directed, is known as the "Contact Person." As soon as possible, a writing acquaintance should be developed with that contact person, or persons, who resides in the vicinity of your proposed trip, knows the region, becomes involved in your plans and needs—in short, a kindred soul.

On our first wilderness trip, we should have had one! Our duffel was piled high on the Red Lake, Ontario, Canada, floating bushplane dock, when a native came along and stopped to chat with us. In exuberant conversation, while awaiting the plane, we explained our proposed route—from the Hudson's Bay Co. Post at Pikangikum to Sandy Lake!

He gasped.

"Do you fellows realize there are seventy-two portages involved?" he asked. "Many of

the narrow streams with windfalls require chopping to get a canoe through!"

He didn't wait for us to recover from our shocked surprise, but in urgent helpfulness cautioned, "Even the Indians wouldn't attempt that back-breaking trip within three weeks."

Mr. Hansen (I believe that was his name) should have been our contact person from the beginning of our planning. During our brief encounter, he helped us evolve a realistic plan. Our itinerary, evolved in the comfort of our homes, was not only unrealistic, but impossible from the most remote concept of canoeing that wilderness. Negotiating a third of the originally planned route was more than adventurous and satisfying.

2. Write to an outfitter asking him about the availability of canoes in the sizes you may need for your party, telling him:

Getting an opinion on a map problem.
JOHN W. MALO PHOTO

a. how many of you will go on the trip;

b. what equipment, gear, and supplies you'd like to have him get ready for you;

c. when you expect to arrive (and how); and

d. what permits, licenses, reservations, fees, if any, will be required.

3. Obtain a map of the area as soon as possible, and study it carefully for:

a. drops in elevation that produce waterfalls and rapids, making portages necessary;

b. the nature of the water—large lakes, narrow streams, white water, etc.;

c. try to picture the land from the map symbols of hills, marsh, and contour; and

d. campsites.

4. A good waterproof map becomes the blueprint of your adventure: make certain that each member of the crew has an exact waterproof copy of the map. In this way, responsibility is shared, for "two minds are better than one." This is especially true when trying to find tricky, concealed outlets from a lake, when trying to avoid going up long dead-end fingers of water, or when navigating large lakes with many islands. The identification of land masses—islands, peninsulas, mainland—offers a challenge that will bring many opinions, and is best decided by all minds.

5. The extent of the route to be followed is an important consideration. It is unrealistic to sit at a table in the comfort of your living room, trace your finger along a map route, and declare, "This is how we'll go!" Paddling the canoe along that same ambitious route will be something else again—with wind, rain, insects, and perhaps numerous portages. Do not be too free with the finger, delineating a back-breaking trip that will become demoralizing.

It's better to plan a shorter trip and have layover days at campsites than a longer trip requiring paddling all day, every day, and having to pitch camp at a new campsite each night.

6. Another item of importance is a sunrise and sunset table for the area to be traveled giving approximate check of time with each passing day. Should watches fail, the canoe party can estimate the time, essential when meeting a scheduled bush plane or train pickup (see Chapter 9).

3

The Quartermaster's Role

THE trip leader serves as the quartermaster for community equipment: first-aid, tool, canoe patch, and sewing kits, insecticides, and the bringing together of all final phases of planning, amassing of community gear, transportation, and departure.

Without such a leader, it is easy for some items to be duplicated, while others may be completely forgotten. In short, the quartermaster assumes the responsibility for details which, if left to the other fellow, may be overlooked.

"MUST" ITEMS

Certain articles that preclude extensive discussion in the planning sessions must be included in the trip cargo.

FIRST-AID KIT AND MANUAL. Include an elastic bandage and Halzone tablets for water

purification, even though you hope neither will be needed.

TOOL KIT. Nails, wire, twine, extra flashlight batteries, wire cutter pliers, small screwdriver and file, hone with a rough and a smooth side to sharpen knives and the ax.

SEWING KIT. Large and small needles, thread, buttons, safety pins, small pair of scissors.

CANOE PATCH KIT. For the wood-canvas canoe: canvas or muslin, ambroid or other quick-drying waterproof cement. For aluminum canoes: cold aluminum in a tube. Adhesive tape, chewing gum, spruce or balsam pitch can be used temporarily. For fiber glass canoes: cloth and bond.

WATERPROOF MATCHES secured in a solid case.

CANDLES. For sustained heat to ignite wet kindling wood, for heat and illumination inside the tent (placed inside a can), friction

19

A molded plastic tote box recently developed by Gerry A. Cunningham of Denver, Colorado. The wanigan-type box pack is the only commercial pack of its kind known to the author.

COURTESY COLORADO OUTDOOR SPORTS CORP.

proofing of tight shoes, for waterproofing of a leaking tent.

INSECTICIDES. The "bug bomb" spray is used in the tent a half hour before retiring. Upon bedding down for the night, for mosquitoes that may have entered, spray again lightly. Breathe through the blanket or your sleeve until the spray has settled. During the day, use the liquid type that is applied to the exposed skin. Inquire in advance about local repellents. In an emergency, use a concoction of water and nicotine from pipe tobacco or from cigars. Soak the tobacco in warm water and apply to the skin. Taking a cue from the animals, mud can be used.

MOSQUITO NETTING. Use Bobbinet, which has a fine mesh that screens out tiny pests. Head nets, used with a broad-brimmed hat, are ideal for trippers with skin sensitivity to repellents.

AX, HATCHET, FOLDING SAW, AND FOLDING SHOVEL.

EXTRA PADDLE FOR EACH CANOE—a traditional safety practice on all trips.

TWO FIFTY-FOOT PAINTERS of one-quarter-inch nylon, or three-eighths-inch manilla rope.

WANIGAN, lightweight storage box.

COOKING KIT with nesting pots and plates. Aluminum foil, paper toweling, and a pair of canvas cooking gloves or mitts.

WATERPROOF MAP FOR EACH MEMBER OF THE CREW. BINOCULARS.

A LIGHTWEIGHT TARP FOR EACH CANOE.

CARRYING YOKES FOR CANOES ON PORTAGES.

INDIVIDUAL DITTY BAGS. Reserve supply of matches, toothbrush (use white soap for tooth paste—saves one article), towel and soap, toilet paper, steel mirror, comb, oil or cream for hands, face, and scalp, extra shoelaces, safety pins, sunglasses, pocketknife, snippers, compass, flashlight, personal medicine, pencils, small notebook, and whistle—and your favorite good luck charm.

The prices of wilderness experiences are relative—depending on what the crew wants. The grandest sights may require back-straining distances and rugged portages, the best fishing spots may also attract mosquitoes, and comfort articles decided on must be weighed against the discomfort of carrying them over the entire route. The loss of city comfort may be the price you'll pay, but it will be worth it—as all great projects have their price.

LUXURY ITEMS OPTIONAL

Each of the trippers' pre-trip planning time will center around the questionable, or the "luxury" items—whether or not to take along the following items:

REFLECTOR OVEN. Its weight and its bulk versus baked bread and cakes.

ONE-BURNER GASOLINE STOVE. Are quick, hot, cooking fires and heating advantages worth the weight attention? Will gathering firewood be a problem?

THE THREE (OR LESS) HP OUTBOARD MOTOR. Augmenting muscle power and extending the range of travel advantages. Don't forget extra shear pins, a spark plug, and a tube of grease.

PHOTOGRAPHIC EQUIPMENT. What items, and should they be limited to one official photographer?

FISHING TACKLE. Limit to five lures that cover the range of surface, medium depth, and deep water (spoons); can be packed in a tin can with pressure top. This selection covers all fishing needs. All the rods are lashed together, or stored in one case to facilitate carrying them over portages.

PAPERBACK BOOKS. How many?

CLOTHING. Restrictions beyond the minimum needs.

AIR OR FOAM RUBBER MATTRESSES. Debate their weight and bulk versus the comfort involved. Be sure to include a patching kit if you take an air mattress.

GIFTS. For friends (Indians in remote areas) along the way: pipe tobacco, cigarettes, snuff, hard candy, gum, .22 rifle bullets, pencils, pens, perfume, soap, simple jewelry, clothing, etc.

THE SHAKEDOWN CRUISE

During the final phase of your planning, you will find it an advantage to test most aspects of your venture with a shakedown cruise.

On it, members of the crew brush up on their canoe strokes, their team paddling, etc.

Should an outboard motor be in the plans, compute the gasoline consumption by checking various speeds for efficiency, which will give you an estimate of the gas needed for the trip, which you will carry—at nine pounds per gallon.

Determine the order of loading the items of your equipment, gear, and duffel.

Test all of your equipment. Unload your canoe, unpack all your gear, pitch your tent, check your sleeping bags.

Use your cooking utensils and test food items, menu, quantities, and other items.

Evaluate the validity of each choice of equipment. Everything on your list must be used and loaded in this shakedown cruise, and MUST EARN ITS PLACE.

If any article is in doubt, the shakedown cruise is the time for pre-testing and final judgment.

The value of a preview of each piece of equipment, gear, clothing, etc., lies in the fact that discovery of needs, of repairs, and of superfluity is best rectified before the trip begins.

PERSONAL GEAR

Follow this principle and procedure, and you'll never be caught under-outfitted. Begin your list with cap or hat, and continue down the body to footwear: a cowboy-size handkerchief, underwear, T shirt, regular long sleeved shirt, suspenders, and belt, trousers, socks and shoes.

Then list a second set of the same items. The second head covering could be a tam, folding cap, or beret, the shirt, perhaps a sweat shirt, the socks and shoes lighter or heavier (to meet different conditions), etc. Far from stores or outfitters, a single pair of shoes can be ruined, a hat blown away and lost, trousers torn, belt broken, etc.

Proper planning of your two sets of clothing assures a margin of safety.

Rain gear, poncho or rain suit, waterproof hat or hood, should protect the entire body. Keep it separate, so it is handy.

Shirts should be of light wool, generously cut, with large pockets. Experts are unanimous in declaring that only wool should be worn.

Socks should be of wool. Wash them daily in mild soap; squeeze dry; do not wring. Do not place wet socks or shoes too near the fire to dry.

Shoes should include ankle-top for rough terrain, canvas for cruising, and moccasins for campsite. Before the trip break new shoes in

The Vagabond Pack, utilizing the mountain backpacking advantages of lightness, comfort, and zippered compartments, is an ideal canoe-camping pack.
COURTESY COLORADO OUTDOOR SPORTS CORP.

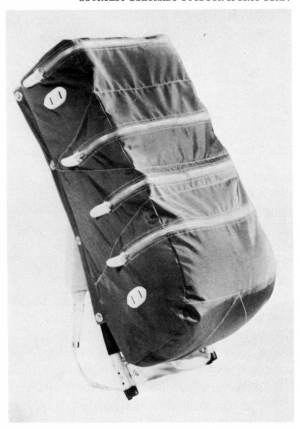

by waxing the tops and walking in them until they fit the contour of the feet. Never take a new pair of shoes on a trip without taking this precaution.

Trousers may be any material but corduroy. Denim, hard-finish cotton, khaki cotton sateen, and water repellent poplin are ideal fabrics, and with large slash pockets make suitable trousers.

Sleeping clothes of cotton "thermal," insulated, fish-net underwear, or the athletic sweat shirt are bulky, but well worth that disadvantage, and one set should be included in each tripper's personal gear, along with his sleeping bag. A good night's sleep is important to the health and temperament of campers.

BACK PACKS. The popularity of packsacks seems to differ by regions, though the traditional ones are the Duluth and Hudson's Bay Packs. The metal frame pack used by the United States Army is ideal for heavy loads, and its increasing popularity comes from lightweight metal construction, snugness that keeps the weight away from the body, allowing for ventilation and coolness, and keeping rough objects from digging into the back.

Mark with India ink (waterproof) everything that can be marked before stowing in packs. Shipping tag labels with strings attached, listing contents, are tied to packs to help find quickly the desired items.

THE TRIPPER GETS READY

The success and enjoyment of the trip will depend on each member of the crew having his clothing, personal items, and equipment ready and delivered at the meeting place on time.

Each crew member should:

1. Attend all planning sessions of the crew;

2. Get a physical check-up if there is any doubt about his bodily condition;

3. If he wears glasses, get a second pair with his prescription, and carry them in a hard case;

4. Get a short, cropped haircut (the day before leaving, if possible);

5. Have prescriptions for personal medication filled, so that an adequate quantity is packed in his ditty bag;

6. Check his sleeping bag, packsacks, and pack boards to make sure they're in perfect condition;

7. Reread one or more of the excellent books on camping and wilderness survival;

8. Be sure he has his own marked maps and compass;

9. Have only the number of paperback books allotted to himself, making sure of no duplication with others;

10. Take his fishing tackle and licenses for each state he plans to enter.

Leave Nothing to Chance

General well-being, good health, and safety are important regardless of circumstances and locale.

The value of trip planning is that "roughing it" does not include enduring discomfort that can be avoided, even in remote areas. One can enjoy reasonable comfort in wilderness living.

Your Crew May Want to Ride a Hobby Horse

Canoeists ambitious enough to embark on a wilderness trip may wish to include activities not usually associated with canoeing, such as

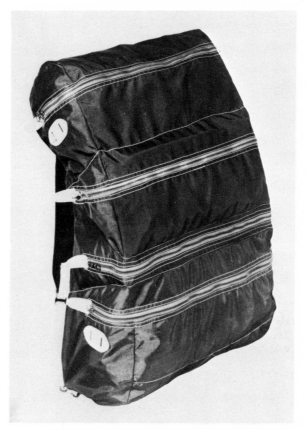

The Traveler Sack fitted to a rigid aluminum frame, with adjustable nylon straps, makes a comfortable rig for long portages, and for extra-heavy weights.
COURTESY COLORADO OUTDOOR SPORTS CORP.

gold panning (see Chapter 11), photography, tape recording, or prospecting. Any equipment and supplies needed for individual or group activity must be carefully considered.

Each member of the crew should carry out any and all responsibilities for the whole crew for which he either volunteers or is assigned.

Check your transportation to the crew's meeting place. No dead car batteries the minute you're supposed to leave!

Part Two

GRUB GUIDELINES AND
THE CAMP KITCHEN

≥ 4 ≥

Wonder Foods
of the Past

GRUB for the modern wilderness canoeist compares favorably with the foods of early wayfarers: the seventeenth-century Voyageurs who spent entire seasons on rivers and in the forests, Kit Carson and Jim Bridges, the Lewis and Clark expedition of two years' duration on water, flatland, and mountain, and the wagon train passengers on their long treks across the prairies—to name a few. Most of them had to carry along their food. Trying to live off the land was risky even in the wild and virgin country.

Then, as now, to sustain bodily needs, nutrition called for a diet of proteins, carbohydrates, fats, fruit, and vegetables. The lack of suitable and consistent refrigeration also complicated their problem. Perishables had to be supplied when the larder diminished: the resources of the region had to be shot, trapped, caught, and harvested for the flesh of animal, wild fowl and fish, for berries,

fruits, and mushrooms; and in dire circumstances, birds' eggs, frogs, crayfish, turtles, and small animals had to serve; in extreme need, even grubs and worms were eaten.

For those "on-the-go" travelers, the problems of preservation by dehydrating food both to maintain its savoriness and to preserve it almost indefinitely had been solved centuries before.

A look at some of their wonder foods should help you discover how they can serve you, the modern canoeist.

Jerky

Jerky (dried beef), one of the most concentrated edibles known to the outdoorsman, has a high nutritional value, lacking only Vitamin C and animal fats.

Almost any meat except pork can be jerked. Originally, venison was most used, but today

27

beef is usually jerked, and is preferred by many.

The name "jerky" comes from the Spanish *charqui*, meaning dried meat, which the Spaniards had adopted from the Indians, who had discovered and perfected the process centuries before.

"Please pass me some of that stuff that won the West," is a jocular comment made by canoeists when jerky is on the menu. And they are not far from wrong. Jerky was a food fuel adopted by early travelers, and the Spaniards, probably the most extensive foot explorers of our continent, used jerky extensively, as did the Mountain Men, the explorers, and the settlers.

How to Jerk Meat

A purposeful pre-canoe-trip project would be to jerk your own beef. This ideal, easy-to-

prepare food staple is time-consuming in preparation, which is why the commercial product is so expensive.

1. Select lean round steak, about a half-inch thick, staying away from expensive cuts which usually are heavily marbled, since fat does not dry well and eventually turns rancid.

2. Trim all fat and remove muscle tissue.

3. Slice the meat into long strips about three-quarters of an inch wide, cutting along the grain, although (because of the anatomical structure of the steak) some of the strips will be cross-grained.

4. Sprinkle the strips liberally with salt and pepper. Oregano, marjoram, basil, and thyme also may be used. You can't overdo the season herbs as the dehydration process weakens their initial flavor.

5. With a meat hammer or the open end of a heavy cup, pound the meat well, but not so hard as to break down the fibers.

Indian jerking moose meat at Little Grand Rapids, Ontario.
JOHN W. MALO PHOTO

6. Turn over the strips and repeat the seasoning and the pounding.

7. Blanch the meat by dipping each strip into very hot water which has been salted and peppered. Ten to fifteen seconds in the water is sufficient time.

8. The actual dehydrating process is now done. Impale one end of each strip on an S-shaped hook (a bent paper clip works fine), and hang out on a line to dry in the sun.

NOTE: When game was plentiful, frontiersmen would stop their other projects and continue with the jerking chore, neither wasting time nor using great imagination, but simply cutting the flesh of buffalo, deer, moose, elk, and caribou into strips and hanging them out to dry upon bushes, clotheslines, or racks. A smudge fire under the meat served the dual purpose of assisting the drying process and helping ward off flies.

9. In warm, dry, sunshiny weather, the jerky will dry in four or five days.

10. If it rains, place a plastic sheet over the drying meat.

11. If flies are a problem, cover the strings of meat with a cheesecloth.

To avoid outdoor drying, lay strips of meat (not touching or overlapping) on a grill. Place the grill over an aluminum foil-lined pan (grill not touching lining), and dry in oven of gas stove with pilot light only, for approximately four days.

Don't despair at the blackish color, the hard texture, and the initial flavor when popping a slice of jerky into your mouth. Chew it as you would leather for a few moments, then through the saliva and the mastication process, the taste of spicy, juicy beefsteak will come through—and you'll be "hooked" on the stuff.

12. Store your jerky in cans with friction tops, and to exclude all air, if necessary, add tape.

When canoeing, it is best to carry jerky in plastic bags, for when packed in this manner, it will neither spoil nor lose its flavoriness, and you'll always have at hand a ready supply of trail food that can be used in many ways.

Several pieces in the mouth with a swig of water activate the taste buds and are a pickup to a fatigued and hungry canoeist.

Jerky can be used to fortify soups and stews, boiled in the water used for noodles, rice, or spaghetti, or thickened with a little flour for a good meat-and-gravy meal.

Pemmican

The early canoeists' contribution to the discovery, exploration, and eventual settlement of the United States and Canada was probably made possible—certainly definitely enhanced—by pemmican, a remarkable energy-giving food borrowed, too, from the Indians. Fur trader Peter Bond, the discoverer of a canoe route up the St. Lawrence River, through the Great Lakes, and then to Lake Athabaska, learned from the Crees and Chipewyans how to make and to use pemmican, which he described as "dry'd meat pounded to a powder and mixed with buffeloes greese."

After his long polar journey, Admiral Robert Peary said: "Of all the foods I am acquainted with, pemmican is the only one that, under appropriate conditions, a man can eat twice a day for three hundred and sixty-five days in a year and have the last mouthful taste as good as the first. . . . Pemmican is the most satisfying food I know."

Pemmican was indispensable to the fur trade and canoe explorers. It was packed in ninety-pound bags, with melted tallow poured over the mixture. Three or four pounds of the highly nutritious food was the daily ration for members of the fur brigades. While paddling, the Voyageurs ate it cold, and at camp added flour and water to it to make a thick, rib-sticking stew called "rubbaboo."

How to Make Pemmican

1. To prepare your own pemmican at home, cut the lean beef into thin slices, and dry over a slow fire, or in the sun, or by freezing.

2. Then pound the meat into a near powder form.

3. Add melted suet and mix together thoroughly and quickly.

Do not use any condiments.

4. The flavor of pemmican comes from adding raisins, dried blueberries, chopped apricots or peaches, or nuts.

5. Two tablespoons of sugar for every pound of meat also can be added.

6. When cool, pack the pemmican in commercial sausage casings or in suitable plastic bags.

Pemmican will keep for months without refrigeration, and indefinitely in a cool, dry place.

It contains all the food essentials to sustain active physical life except Vitamin C (as jerky), and since a healthy man can survive for fifty or sixty days without that vitamin, there is no problem for the canoeist on a wilderness trip: furthermore, Tang and Hemo, beverages mentioned later, are rich in the vitamin. No need to go into the forest for rose hips or cattail root.

Pinole

Pinole, very similar to pemmican, is an ideal emergency food. It, too, comes from the Indians—the southwestern Indians in the United States and Mexico—is easily prepared, won't spoil, and will sustain the canoeist in good health for a long while. As then, the basic corn meal can be supplemented with bits of fish, meat, dried fruit, or nuts. A handful of pinole, washed down with water, will sustain a person all day.

The basic ingredient is corn:

1. Parch a pint of kernel corn in a hot oven at 350 degrees.

2. When completely browned, not burned, sprinkle evenly over the top two tablespoonfuls of brown sugar.

3. Then place in the oven again for the sugar to melt and coat each kernel.

4. Cool the mixture.

5. Grind into a meal with a home food grinder.

6. Pack in plastic bags.

7. For security, place the bags in an extra canvas bag for safe packing in a packsack.

In early history, pinole, an easily prepared survival food, enabled the Indians and the Spanish Conquistadors to traverse vast regions of wilderness.

Smoked Fish

Another wilderness food staple that can be enjoyed without refrigeration is smoked fish. The abundance of fish, like game, seems to occur in cycles. Should your wilderness trip take you to prolific waters and you catch more fish than can be used at the moment, smoking is the answer if you wish to preserve them. As in jerky preparation, curing fish is a matter of smoking or drying out the moisture:

1. Clean the fish, remove heads, and cut the belly side up to the backbone—to the skin.

2. Open up the fish so that two flat slabs, butterfly-type wings, are spread apart, held together only by the thin skin acting as a hinge.

3. After the above preparation, soak the fish overnight, in a strong solution of salt water.

4. Prior to the smoking chore, wipe the fish dry.

Poplar Hill Indians drying fish for the winter trapping season.
JOHN W. MALO PHOTO

5. Rig a long pole, braced horizontally, about four feet above the fire. Over the pole, drape the slabs of fish.

For the fire, use any wood, but take care not to use the resinous evergreens. Green wood about five inches in diameter, split into quarters, is best encouraged by periodically adding small branches to keep the smudge fire going. Keep the heat low, controlled, and continuous. The smudge fire requires constant attention to keep the fire from blazing up. A pail of water and a cup should be placed nearby to douse a hot, smokeless fire. Should other activities, such as fishing, exploring, sleeping, take you away from tending the fire, allow it to go out and start it again when convenient.

A crude cover (tarp or bark) surrounding the rig, open at the top, will confine the smoke and direct it upward through the fish, at the same time keeping off the rain and the dew.

Living today as their forefathers did hundreds of years ago, wilderness Indians in parts of Canada construct their smokehouses of large strips of birch or aspen bark shaped into a cone-like or wigwam structure. Racks of green alder or willow (bottomland trees),

two to three feet high, upon which the fish are placed, are built inside. The crossbars are nailed or wired one inch apart, to prevent the smoked fish from dropping through. One, two, or three drying shelves are used, depending on the size of the catch.

The Cree Indians at Poplar Hill, Ontario, Canada, drape the cleaned, split fish slabs on a line strung between trees, one-half dangling on either side, and through the heat of the sun, the fish are dried. All summer long, their settlement is crisscrossed with lines supporting drying fish. Husky dogs, used by the Indians on their fall and winter hunting and trapping expeditions, eat a prodigious amount of food, and it takes all summer to net and to prepare an adequate supply of smoked fish for them.

In all fish-smoking projects, the curing time depends on the efficiency of the smokehouse, the humidity, and on the thickness of the fish. After eight hours (or more) of curing, the fish dehydrate to a crumbling texture, golden brown in color, and wrinkled.

The advantage of tending the smokehouse is the occasional tasting ritual.

5

Grub
and Menus

MODERN scientists, spurred by national security needs and space exploration, have greatly extended the range of processed foods which require neither refrigeration nor special precautions.

From the primitive processing of food, discussed in Chapter 4, we have progressed to powdered, concentrated, freeze-dried, irradiated, "wet pack," and dehydrated techniques.

For those canoeists who feel more comfortable on the trail with a general menu of meals, the blending of the old and the new foodstuffs is included.

MORNING MEALS

Breakfast need be neither much different from nor less palatable and nourishing in the wilderness than at home.

The morning meal is considered by nutritionists to be the most important meal of the day. Regardless of eating habits (sometimes no breakfast), the canoeist is urged to eat a hearty morning meal—the better to engage in the activities of the day.

Juices, hot and cold cereals, bacon, scrambled eggs, pancakes, French toast, beverage of one's choice—all are available and easily prepared for canoeists.

Bacon in three forms can be included—slab, canned pre-fried, and pressed bars:

BACON SLABS keep better than sliced bacon, and in addition to savoriness, supply fat in which to fry other foods. Slab bacon should be well smoked, placed in a cheesecloth bag, and sliced as needed.

Dice and use in omelets, with beans, noodles, etc.

After several days, should the slab bacon

become green with mold, scrape off with a knife blade or wash with vinegar.

The bacon can be resmoked from time to time by hanging over low smoke fire.

Compute the slab bacon ration at one pound per week, per person. Because Canadian bacon contains less fat than the ordinary bacon, some campers prefer it.

CANNED BACON, with all its fat fried out, is expensive, but results in pure bacon strips that can be used in many ways.

THE BACON BAR is pre-fried bacon pressed into a concentrated bar, three ounces being equivalent to one pound of cooked bacon. The bar can be crumbled on potatoes and beans, in eggs, and in flapjack batter, or carried in the pocket and eaten on the trail.

DRIED FRUITS (which have been soaked overnight) are stewed, and sugar added at the last moment for a delicious first course. If stewed fruit is on the menu the previous night, to save time, prepare enough then for the next morning's meal. Practically all fruits can be found in dry form: apples, apricots, bananas, dates, figs, pears, prunes, etc.

Dried fruits can be used in many ways: stewed and seasoned, eaten raw while on the go, chopped fine and added as ingredients to oatmeal, pancakes, and baked goods.

Prunes represent a popular camp food because of their laxative action, and should be used as often as necessary. Cereals, such as oatmeal, corn meal, cream of wheat, and other grain foods furnish concentrated nourishment, and can be made palatable in many ways: with honey or brown sugar for sweetening, the addition of raisins, fig or date chips, berries, cinnamon, etc.

CORN MEAL contains potassium, and can be used as a cereal or as pancakes. Several cold cereals on the market, though bulky in their boxes, are rich in vitamins, and furnish all a canoeist needs for a day's paddling or hiking.

There are instant wheat and rice cereals on the market (in cartons containing individual serving packets) needing only hot water stirred into them.

EGGS packed in plastic cartons are used by some outfitters, so that campers can enjoy the benefit of whole eggs. Formerly, they were also packed in friction-top cans with sawdust or shredded paper to prevent breakage. The bother of protecting whole eggs is probably acceptable for a few days, but on an extended trip, they must be replaced by powdered eggs. The statistic—one-half pound of powdered eggs equals two dozen fresh eggs—immediately shows the value of the powdered egg product. For menu considerations, a tablespoon of powdered egg added to two tablespoons of water gives the equivalent of one egg. The one-to-two ratio is easily remembered. Eggs of good quality, in their powdered form, can be served in a variety of ways to please the most finicky eater.

SCRAMBLED EGGS are good made by this recipe: one-quarter cup powdered egg, two tablespoons powdered milk, one teaspoon salt, one-half teaspoon pepper, one and a half cups water. Thoroughly mix all the dry ingredients, then add the water and blend into a smooth paste. Pour the batter into the frying pan containing a little hot grease. A controlled fire of embers will not scorch the eggs, which should be stirred and removed while of a moist and soft consistency.

With this simple basic recipe, a little imagination used by any wilderness cook will make him a culinary artist: 1. The addition of a little baking powder will fluff up the eggs. 2. Grated cheese, dried mushrooms, onion flakes, bacon or lunch meat squares can be used so that no two egg preparations will be alike.

AN OMELET FOR TWO CANOEISTS: Mix six tablespoons of powdered eggs, two tablespoons of powdered milk, and one cup (sixteen tablespoons) of water. Add one-half teaspoon salt, and a little pepper. Beat the mixture with a fork until the consistency is the same as fresh eggs.

Prepare the skillet with a lump of butter or bacon fat, pour in the mixture, and stir with a fork. When it resembles scrambled eggs, stop stirring and leave the skillet on a low, even heat until the bottom of the omelet sets firmly (like a pancake). Run a spatula under the omelet and fold one half of it over the other half. Serve. Fillings may be of vegetables (two tablespoons dehydrated, prepared beforehand) such as peas, carrots, pepper flakes, celery flakes, dehydrated onions, or dried mushrooms.

FRENCH TOAST served hot with syrup and bacon makes good eating, and is easy to prepare, as well as being a use for bread that has become hard and dry. For eight slices, mix into a consistency as for scrambled eggs; six tablespoons powdered eggs, six tablespoons water, twelve tablespoons powdered milk, salt and pepper. Soak the bread slices well on both sides. Fry in butter or bacon fat until crisp and golden brown.

REGULAR TOAST is easily made on an open fire: level off a portion of hot coals, drop on them a slice of bread and lift it off immediately. Repeat with the other side. Within twenty seconds or so, you have delicious toast.

PANCAKES can be made from mixes that are so numerous, delicious, and satisfying that the camper need not start from scratch with ingredients to fry up a stack of this traditional outdoor favorite. Fortify the batter of commercial mixes (buckwheat, corn meal, oatmeal, wheat hearts, etc.) with powdered eggs, berries, and milk. Stir the flour and water lightly to a relatively thin batter to make more palatable, thin pancakes that fry faster. Thick pancakes gag the throat and are harder to digest.

The bottom of the frying pan must be scoured clean and be well greased with butter or other cooking fat over the entire bottom. With a ladle, drop the batter on the pan, allowing plenty of space between cakes. Flip each over with a spatula when the pancake turns golden brown on the edges and bubbles on top. Keep a warm plate near the fire for the finished cakes. Stagger them about the plate; stacking one on top of the other makes them soggy. Serve with syrup, jelly (available in tubes), or honey.

SYRUPS in many flavors are available in dry form, requiring only the addition of water. Should your syrup rations be used up, two substitutes can be quickly concocted: butterscotch, by mixing one cup of brown sugar and three tablespoons butter with one-half cup of water, and boiling for five minutes; and maple syrup, by using one-half cup maple sugar, one-half cup white sugar, one-half cup water, and boiling.

COOKING FATS are a constant concern for camp cooks. Grease from slab bacon (a continuing supply) should be saved in a screw- or friction-top can. Butter, lard, and vegetable shortenings come in cans and keep well. Corn and peanut oil, preferred by many canoeists, can be placed in plastic containers which pack and carry well on the trail.

BEVERAGES IN DEHYDRATED FORM—powder and crystals—need but the addition of water to return to their original form.

POWDERED WHOLE MILK, obtainable from your local bakery, is prepared by adding one cup of powdered milk to three and a half cups water, to make one quart of fresh milk. Add a pinch of salt and a tablespoon of sugar, place the mixture in a closed can or pot, and shake vigorously. To aerate the milk, then pour it back and forth from one pot to another. Leave it to set for a while, as the taste of powdered milk improves with time. Mix a batch the previous night for morning use. For extended trips (beyond three weeks), powdered skim milk should be used as it does not get rancid as whole-milk powder may. I have seen the children of Hudson's Bay Post personnel in Canadian wildernesses, rosy-cheeked and healthy, who'd never tasted milk from a bottle, and were thriving on powdered milk and drinking it with relish.

ORANGE, TOMATO, AND GRAPEFRUIT crystals, with the addition of water, make good first course breakfast juices.

LIME AND LEMON crystals made into a drink are ideal for the long, hot days when thirst is an ever-present condition.

MIXES RICH IN VITAMIN C: Various mixes, Tang in particular, are rich in Vitamin C, as is Hemo, and are ideal for supplementing diet.

COFFEE, the traditional wake-up beverage, is best pot-brewed—in deference to camping lore. Add the ground coffee to boiling water (the few grains slipping between the fingers onto the fire give an aromatic preview of what's to come). One heaping teaspoon of coffee per cup is a good starting point. Coffee drinkers have diverse tastes, and the cook soon adjusts to them with a satisfactory blend. As soon as the boiling coffee is brewed to an opaque brown, remove it from the fire. To settle the grounds add some cold water, or insert a cold knife blade or ladle, which tends to send the grounds quickly to the bottom.

INSTANT COFFEE: some should be included as a back-up ration to the regular supply. It is lightweight and convenient, and some may prefer it on the whole trip. Decaffeinated coffee, coffee with acid removed, freeze-dried, etc., are obtainable in individual packets, needing only boiling water added in the cup.

COCOA OR INSTANT CHOCOLATE MILK is best bought in packages which include all ingredients—cocoa or chocolate, powdered milk, and sugar. The packet, emptied into a cup of near-boiling water and stirred, makes a quick and satisfying drink—any time of the day.

TEA as a beverage is more universally used (probably) than is coffee. Should you use the services of an Indian guide in Canada or Maine, his trip will be spoiled and you will be talked about if there's no tea in the packsack. When Canadian visitors drop in at your campsite, the absence of tea will not endear your party, nor will it cement international relations: tea with cookies, muffins, or biscuits comprises the traditional good-neighbor refreshment.

Tea gourmets differ on how tea should be brewed, though most agree that campers boil the leaves too long. Administer the boiling water to dry tea and set it beside the fire to steep for five minutes. Some prefer to bring along their favorite brand of tea in bags or tins. There's instant tea that may be made with cold water, tea with lemon, tea with orange, etc.—for variety, should your crew prefer.

SASSAFRAS TEA, made from the root of the plant, has served as a tonic since pioneer days. Dig up the main root of the small, shrub-like tree, wash and dry it. Slice off pieces of the juicy bark and place in a pot, cover with a cup or two of water, and bring to a boil. For a saffron-colored tea of delightful fragrance, take the pot from the fire, cover, and allow to stand for at least five minutes. Few woodsy aromas compare with it. The roots are not quickly expendable; hang them up to dry and use them over and over until all the juicy sap has been used. Buying sassafras roots can be a mission in itself. Country stores, specialty food shops, and some chain stores sell them, in season.

THE EARLY RISER (there's one in every group) makes the fire, gets the water and places it on the fire—which is good organization. Boiling water is a necessary breakfast preparation—for beverage, hot cereal, etc. The "late sleepers" are grateful for the extra "sack time."

MIDDAY MEALS

The canoeist can take a clue from the Canadian fishing guide's method of serving a shore lunch for the midday meal. It is quick and efficient, taking away little time from fishing. At a suitable site, he immediately slants a pole over the quickly made fire, braces it with stones and sets on a pot of water. Then he filets the fish (walleye, smallmouth bass, or lake trout), wipes them dry, and places the frying pan, half filled with grease, over the coals. The fishermen, under the guide's direction, open the canned vegetables and place them (in their original tins) on the edge of the fire. Before long, the water (for coffee or tea) is boiling, the fish are sizzling, and the vegetables are warm. For dessert, fruit and large cookies.

There's always the precaution against "poor fishing": in the packsack are tins of canned meat.

Fish dinner in the wilderness is quite logical, for many times fishing is on the program, and frying the catch makes good sense. If you don't like fish, try eating a walleye, trout, or perch, freshly caught, firm and cold, immediately killed, cleaned, and fried. It makes believers out of non-believers.

Preparation is the answer: with cloth or paper towel wipe the flesh of the fish dry. The peanut or vegetable oil or shortening, the lard or bacon fat, should cover half the fish, be sizzling hot before receiving the fish. The hot fat immediately seals the pores of the fish in a sizzling sound. Fry one side, then gently turn over to brown the other. Stack the fish on paper toweling to absorb the remaining grease. There is never a fish odor connected with the whole procedure.

NOTE: The addition of many pieces of fish lowers the temperature of the grease: therefore, after each addition, wait until the grease is sizzling again before adding the next piece. The grease does not permeate the fish when it is dry and the grease is sizzling hot. That's the main trick in properly frying fish.

Aluminum foil enables the cook to broil fish. After fileting, rub salt, pepper, and butter or margarine over and inside the fish, then place it on a sheet of foil and crimp the edges into an air-tight covering over the entire fish. Place the package on a bed of hot coals—usually ten minutes or more, depending on size. The makeshift oven captures the fish juices, and the butter permeates the succulent flesh. A little lemon juice heightens the savoriness of fish. Rice and spinach or potatoes, peas, and carrots are good side dishes.

Should your catch exceed immediate needs, preserve it for a few days: wipe dry, remove gills, wipe off slime, and wrap the fish in paper towels or ferns. Never wash the fish or wrap in any airtight material. Hang the packed fish in the open shade on the breezy side of camp.

More often than having a fish fry on shore, the wilderness canoeist—on the go—will take his lunch on the run, sometimes in the canoe, by eating a handful of pemmican, as did the Voyageurs when there was an urgency to their schedules. The advantages of a cold lunch are many: no fire to make, no cooking utensils to store and wash, no time wasted, but much saved.

SANDWICHES for the trail, using pumpernickel bread, rye biscuits, hard crackers, pilot bread, or morning pancakes, can be filled with a variety of foodstuffs: peanut butter and jelly; peanut butter, chopped raisins and figs; peanut butter and chopped, fried bacon; cheese and chopped bacon; salami or dried sausage; tinned luncheon meat, canned beef or ham; chopped figs and nuts with a little bit of peanut butter and a dash of lemon juice; any leftover fish, by adding a few drops of lemon juice; scrambled eggs with bacon squares.

With sandwiches, use these foodstuffs as dessert on a rotation basis throughout the week: dried fruits, peanuts or mixed nuts, chocolate bars, malted milk tablets, cheese, and hard candy.

Beverages of citric derivation are the recommended drinks for the heat of the day.

ON COLD DAYS, or when the group is campbound, the bother of preparing a hot meal may be welcome. As a starter, soups can be enriched by adding bouillon cubes, broken spaghetti, noodles, Parmesan cheese (especially with onion soup), and dried mushrooms. Some tested soup combinations are green pea with cream of celery; onion and chicken gumbo with grated Parmesan cheese; vegetable with cream of mushroom; carrots and peas added to vegetable soup; and chicken broth with cream of mushroom soup.

A hot sandwich is easily made: place ham, corned beef, or cheese between two slices of bread; soak both sides of the sandwich in a beaten egg batter; season with salt and pepper; and fry on both sides in plenty of bacon fat until brown. Serve while hot.

For dessert serve cookies or instant pudding and a hot beverage of eaters' choice.

EVENING MEALS

Days are long in the Northland during the canoe-camping season, and often the last meal of the day is served quite late. Experience dictates that the meal best be prepared and served, the dishes washed, and all provisions secured before sunset—giving ample time for evening fishing and for scrounging firewood for the evening campfire and for the next morning's breakfast fire.

SOUPS. Flavorful soups with good body, served with crackers or coarse bread, liberally spread with butter or margarine, constitute a meal. Soups can be given more body by adding powdered milk, powdered potato, salt pork, or commercial, dry soup stock. Discretion is the word here: don't overpower the soup.

Flavor can be imparted through the addition of tomato paste, bouillon cubes, onion flakes, bacon fat, butter, salt and pepper. The flavoring agents should be compatible with the original soup.

The advantages of modern food processing are indicated by the dinner-meal offerings of reputable companies that have served canoeists in a most delicious way.

KISKY FOODS, INC., 1829 N.E. Albert St., Portland, Oregon 97211, touts in Dinner No. 1, cream of potato soup, spaghetti dinner with beef, biscuit bread, fruit spread, coconut pudding, and raspberry punch. Dinner No. 2, tomato soup, hunter's stew with beef, trail tac, apple butter spread, butterscotch instant pudding, and orange punch.

DRI LITE FOODS, 11333 Atlantic Ave., Lynwood, California 90262, offers for dinner, meat balls and mashed potatoes, brown gravy, trail cookies, apple d'lite, and cocoa; Spanish rice with bacon, golden bantam corn, pilot biscuit, instant jelly, and chocolate malt drink.

CHUCK WAGON FOODS, 176 Oak St., Newton, Massachusetts 02164, offers beef bouillon, chicken à la king, trail toast, gel dessert, cookies, and fruit drink; chicken broth, beef and vegetable dinner, applesauce, biscuits, and milk.

AD. SEIDEL AND SONS, INC., 2323 Pratt Blvd., Elk Grove Village, Illinois 60007, offers beef hash, applesauce, butterscotch cream dessert, and sweet milk cocoa; chicken noodle soup, ham 'n potato dinner, vanilla extract pudding, punch beverage.

PERMA-PAK, 40 East 2430 South, Salt Lake City, Utah 84115, offers chili with beans, protein crumbles, Yukon biscuits, gingerbread, and vanilla shake; chicken rice dinner, biscuits, chips, green peas, honey, and beverage.

THE BOY SCOUTS TRADING POST, with branches in most large cities, also supplies a variety of dehydrated foods.

NOTE: Even though food is completely supplied by food companies, these items should be added: butter or margarine, salt pork, salt, pepper, and SUGAR.

COST OF GRUB

The cost of meals varies with the choice of foods. Ham or bacon with eggs for breakfast cost more than a bowl of oatmeal. The total cost for a trip (from the above companies) will be $1.50 to $1.75 per person, per day, for well-balanced meals, including meat, eggs, and other protein foods.

Without meat, the cost drops to approximately 40¢ per meal.

There's no spoilage, and the processed fruits and vegetables are already peeled, pared, and pitted.

The wholesome dinners, as breakfasts and lunches, given above, are representative of a great deal of research in food processing and packaging. Through constant research, every meal provides appetizing eating, and is well balanced, having flavor comparable to home-cooked foods.

The procedure for preparation of each meal is included in every trail kit, and each meal (for four to eight persons) is packaged separately, ready for the canoe trip.

All meals are sealed in waterproof polyethylene bags, and in case of unexpected dunking will float. The bags are readily disposed of—by burning—or they can be used as handy carriers for soap, matches, compass, film, and what-have-you.

The U.S. Department of Agriculture's recent edition of *Composition of Foods* gives assurance that proteins, sugars, carbohydrates, minerals, vitamins, and fats are not removed when the foods are processed.

Buy in Advance

The remarkable advantage of commercially processed foods is that they can be ordered weeks in advance of the trip: in fact, they can be ordered during the winter for summer use, which spreads the extensive chore of logistics.

The meal packets can be broken down and grouped together so that meals for each day (Monday's, for example) can be packed together in a breakfast-lunch-dinner combination to be pulled out on the trail and save a lot of probing the packs.

Reasonable quantities of food, gasoline, oil —for the tourists' use—are granted free entry by Canada, such as two days' food (per person) and gas for 300 miles of motoring.

Counting Calories

These guidelines for grub planning are important:

1. Active teen-agers require 3,700 to 4,600 calories per day—compared to the housewife's 2,300.

2. Growing boys can play havoc with a grub list if trip planning does not allow for extra food.

3. In computing food needs from commercial sources, buy four servings for three boys, for each meal.

4. The snacks mentioned in midday meals can be rationed out, now and then, to active youths who need to nibble constantly.

5. If a trip becomes difficult and exhausting, the food requirements for all campers can double or triple.

6. On extended canoe trips, because of its bulk an adequate supply of bread cannot be

transported. After using the original ration, it will be necessary to bake in camp. Bread mixes can be baked in a reflector oven, a covered skillet, in an open skillet, by using foil, or between aluminum foil pie tins held together with spring-type clothes pins.

Prepared mixes containing all the necessary ingredients for baking bread, muffins, cookies, corn bread, biscuits, etc., are a boon to camp cooks.

The collapsible, portable, REFLECTOR OVEN is a most efficient piece of kitchen equipment. The two hinged sheets of polished metal concentrate the heat to the baking tray in the middle. Always place the oven with its back to the wind, to shield the fire and to prevent ashes from blowing into the batter.

OPEN-SKILLET BAKING is used for camp bread (bannock). The dry mixture is made into a pliable dough—using the greased skillet after the morning bacon has been cooked. Prop up the skillet at an angle, with rocks or a green stick, in front of the fire. Keep the skillet on the windward side of the fire. Turn over the loaf when done on one side. During baking time, finish camp chores, and when it's time to move, the bannock is done. After cooling, place it in a pot to keep it from being crushed in the pack.

FRYING, which can place a burden on the digestive system, is frequently over-used in camp cookery; in practice, too often fried foods are apt to absorb too much fat. As with frying fish, discussed earlier, for effective searing which seals in the juices without grease absorption, the food placed in the skillet should be dry, the grease hot. Wipe fried foods, especially bacon, with paper toweling to remove excess grease.

There is a point in time on extended canoe trips when a psychological lift is needed. The morale booster, besides some special activity, can often be gustatory in nature. "The way to a man's heart . . ." etc. We used all day

suckers once, and on another trip sparklers to celebrate the Fourth of July.

After many days on the trail, a strong hunger develops for leafy vegetables and citrus fruits—a common experience among sailors at sea. A small head of cabbage or two can be stowed (in cloth) without difficulty, and should be carried as long as possible. Check it from day to day, peel off the dry leaves, and it will be possible to serve it as a special treat many days after launching. Serve it raw as a salad, boiled in quarters, stewed with meat, or chopped for soups. The bulk in the diet will be relished. The same is true of lemons and oranges: hold onto them as long as possible, then when that peculiar hunger develops, surprise the group, and you'll be surprised when they eat peels and all.

SURVIVAL KIT. For wilderness trips, a survival kit is very much in order. Chuck Wagon Foods offers such a kit (11 ounces—750 calories) in a compact waterproof package with these items: pemmican, chocolate, candy, fire starter, matches, toilet tissue, water purification tablets, plastic water bag, razor blade, Band-aids, aluminum foil, compass, and a *Survival Instruction Booklet*. The kit lasts for two years without deterioration, and if unused on the first trip, can be taken along any season during that time.

Perma-Pak offers a chow belt, weighing two pounds, with a three-day food supply. The belt is divided into seven pouches, and ties comfortably around the waist or over the shoulder. The chow belt lends itself to extended exploration or prospecting trips, or when away from camp on various missions.

Even though processed foods today are superb—and all outdoorsmen are thankful—new processes are constantly being discovered. For space flight needs, the astronauts eat from plastic tubes such meals as tuna salad, chicken salad, and ham salad, spread on crumbling bread. Radiation-preserved food is on the threshold of being available commercially. The federal Food and Drug Administration has already cleared bacon, potatoes, and wheat flour; and scientists are working on oranges, onions, fish, ham, and other foods. The atomic radiation process eliminates refrigeration. Packaged steaks, for example, could be sold from grocery shelves,

and fresh fruit seasons could be extended almost indefinitely.

When the crew is ready to take off, to make the load as comfortable as possible, stow the heaviest foods at the bottom of the packsack and place clothes against the front side that rests against your back.

6

Fires,
Firewood, and
Kitchen Devices

"EXTREME CAUTION" is the warning to canoe-campers in wilderness areas because of the resinous nature of coniferous trees growing in abundance there.

Pines, for instance, after becoming heated can catch fire. Their green needles burn quickly, as if doused with gasoline, and the flames, carried upward—with or without wind —jump in seconds from treetop to treetop, burning quickly up a rise or across the land.

A forest fire beyond control is the result!

In the wilderness, fires, feeding on the thick carpet of accumulated humus, can creep along over or under the ground. Even after being doused with water, a fire can travel and smolder beneath the surface, grow and ignite favorable combustible leaves or pine needles, to flare up into flame when the air requirement is present.

Your control of your fire(s) is the prime requisite in wild camping areas. Before you lay any fire: clean all debris from your proposed cooking area, scraping away humus, roots, leaves, needles, and grass until bare soil, rock, gravel, or sand is reached. Then build the cooking fire.

In well-traveled areas, often the location of your cooking fire has been pre-determined, but in wilderness areas you will have to contrive one. Simplicity is the rule for the canoeist on the go. The elaborate Chippewa kitchen is not for the one- or two-night stays at a campsite.

I have never found stone arrangements for fire to my liking. They take too long to construct, are uneven, and too often the stones burst (from trapped steam) and send chips flying to smother the fire and to tumble the pots they support.

The best arrangement is the simplest, as illustrated by the hunter's or trapper's fire: two angled logs (four to six inches in diameter) laid on the ground, the widest open end being toward the wind, and as wide as possible to hold your largest pot. Trim the logs on the top side with an ax, so that pots will be less likely to upset. The fire is confined by the logs, and the heat is efficiently directed to the underside of pots and pans. Their ends can be propped up with a stick or stone to

THE VERSATILE CHIPPEWA KITCHEN
FOR PERMANENT CAMPS

A BUCKET OF WATER BOILING,
SIMMERING SOUP, AND FISH FRYING
OVER A HUNTER'S FIRE

admit more air if combustion of fuel is inadequate.

Fuel is easily added from either end, and ventilation can be abetted, cowboy style, with the swish of a hat.

Place green saplings across the logs to accommodate small pots. Should a strong wind whip up, a log or tarp wall arrangement can be placed across the opening to hold the fire in check.

The addition of a crane and/or dingle stick, from which pothooks can hold utensils any desired height above the fire, rounds out the efficient arrangement.

Fires require (in sequence) tinder, kindling, and fuel wood—and all should be on hand before you strike the match. To start the fire, use natural tinder—fuzz sticks—cedar bark and/or birch bark, which, due to the oil in their bark, will burn even when damp. Pine twigs sliced down the middle, slivers of shavings from evergreens which are saturated with pitch, are tinder possibilities.

Build up the fire by adding kindling (which is thin sticks or dead branches split in two to expose the inner core). Then feed fuel wood into the fire. For this, the wood from a standing dead tree, three to four inches in diameter, is ideal, and a supply is at hand to keep the fire going. Place pots and pans on the fire after the blazing wood has been reduced to a bed of coals.

In strong winds, use the trench fire.

For heat reflecting needs (warmth and baking), use the reflector fire.

Use the tepee style for campfires: however, usually the tepee-style fire is the starter for all types of fires.

For broiling over hot coals, use the log-cabin style.

A little knowledge of the best kinds of wood to use, should there be a choice, will help to assure the type of combustion needed for various cooking and heating needs.

VARIETY OF POT HOLDERS WITH
CRANE ARRANGEMENT

Wanigan

Many backwoodsmen use a versatile kitchen box, known as the wanigan, cassette, or chuck box, as a handy storage bin.

The wanigan must be custom built, and can be constructed by fitting a lid to an apple box or orange crate, approximately 24x18x16 inches in size, and attaching soft handles of leather or rope to the ends. Empty beer cases which are tough and semi-waterproof (and with handles) are also used. Clever craftsmen make their homemade creations quite fancy with compartments, linings, bright finishes, etc.

Foods, such as breakfast pancakes, soups, honey in upright containers, to be used for lunch along the trail, fried fish, cake, etc., are transported in the wanigan without crushing or spilling. Cameras, instruments, utensils, medicines—any breakable or delicate item— can be safely stowed in the firm container. On portages, the wanigan is carried with a tump-line, on top of the packsack or lashed to the pack board. It's a bit awkward, but the advantages of this packing contrivance offset its disadvantages.

Clothesline

Hang dish cloths, towels, and laundry on a clothesline placed high enough so that the tallest camper can walk under it without losing his hat. Keep the line away from well-trod paths, and if you must put it where it may be a hazard, keep a towel or other white cloth attached to it for after-dark visible warning.

VARIETY OF DINGLE STICKS—
SINGLE POT HOLDERS

REFLECTOR FIRE FOR REFLECTOR OVEN

SECURING FOOD AGAINST ANIMALS AND OTHER PESTS

Good Housekeeping

I have often pondered how, with the hundreds of square miles of wilderness they have to scout, a fly or a mosquito can so quickly find a newly pitched camp. I have actually heard of campers being driven off a campsite by a plague of flies. The answer is obvious. Food! Unwashed dishes, exposed syrup, sugar, jam, candy, etc., immediately attract flies by the hundreds.

The use of plastic bags, tight-fitting tins, and the observation of the rules of good house-keeping keep away the flies, or fail to attract them.

There's always the temptation to set out nut, raisin, and candy morsels for those attractive little neighbors—squirrels, chipmunks, lemmings, and birds—but that hospitality also brings uninvited guests—raccoons, porcupines, skunks, AND BEARS!

The black bear, inhabiting areas where canoeists travel, probably having had experience with discarded tins not burned out, connects tin cans with food and actually raids packsacks, tears them open, pierces the cans with his teeth, and sucks out the contents.

Animal pests differ by locale and season: porcupines may be a problem in the Wisconsin forests, the black bear in Canada, the raccoon along more southern river bottoms, etc. (see Chapter 15).

NOTE: A question to ask your contact person while formulating trip plans is, "What is the animal-pest situation?"

Provide a Cache for Grub

Although tin cans and plastic containers help keep down the odor of food, in spite of them

RATINGS FOR FIREWOOD

	NAME OF TREE	RELATIVE AMOUNT OF HEAT	EASY TO BURN	EASY TO SPLIT	POPS OR THROWS SPARKS	MAKES HEAVY SMOKE	GENERAL RATING AND REMARKS
BROADLEAF	Ash, red oak, white oak, beech, birch, hickory, hard maple, pecan, dogwood.	High	Yes	Yes	No	No	Excellent.
	Soft maple, cherry, walnut.	Medium	Yes	Yes	No	No	Good.
	Elm, sycamore, gum.	Medium	Medium	No	Medium	No	Fair
	Aspen, basswood, cottonwood.	Low	Yes	Yes	Medium	No	Fair — but good for kindling.
	Chestnut, yellow-poplar.	Low	Yes	Yes	Medium	Yes	Poor.
NEEDLELEAF	Southern yellow pine, Douglas fir.	High	Yes	Yes	Yes	No	Good but smoky.
	Cypress, redwood.	Medium	Medium	Yes	Medium	No	Fair.
	White cedar, western red cedar, eastern red cedar.	Medium	Yes	Yes	Medium	Yes	Good—excellent for kindling.
	Eastern white pine, western white pine, sugar pine, ponderosa pine, true firs.	Low	Medium	Yes	Medium	No	Fair — good kindling.
	Tamarack, larch.	Medium	Yes	Yes	Medium	Yes	Fair.
	Spruce.	Low	Yes	Yes	Medium	Yes	Poor.

FROM *The Log*, AN EXPLORERS JOURNAL, WINTER 1970, USED BY PERMISSION.

grub supplies are raided, so that some kind of food cache or other protection against undesirable ground-crawling pests and larger marauders must be provided.

The usual method of caching food simply is to suspend it out of reach—ten to fifteen feet above the ground. The green-sapling cache is made by bending over a small tree, attaching the plastic bag to its branches and allowing the sapling to snap back into place.

The tree-limb cache utilizes a large branch as a pulley. Tie the bag of food to one end of a rope, a rock to the other end, which you

OVER THE BRANCH CACHE

A half hitch

Two half hitches

Clove hitch

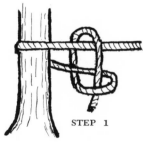

STEP 1

STEP 2

Slip knot or teamster's hitch

Timber hitch

Bowline

Taut-line hitch

Barrel hitch (for cache)

SOME HANDY HITCHES

toss over the limb; haul up the bag. Fasten the free end of the rope around the tree trunk, using a couple of half hitches.

The St. Andrew's cross cache is fashioned by lashing two poles securely together to form a cross. At each of the four ends, balance and secure various packages of food. Tie

the supporting rope at the intersection of the cross members. The swaying action of the cache discourages prowling animals—and ants, too!

You can hang up the wanigan as well as covered pots and the plastic bags.

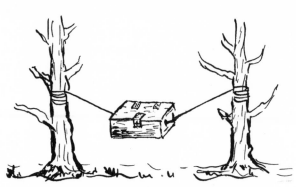

WANIGAN HUNG BETWEEN TREES

ST. ANDREW'S CROSS CACHE

TEPEE CACHE

TREE CACHE

Dining out in an atmosphere of serenity after pitching camp.
MICHIGAN TOURIST COUNCIL PHOTO

KEEPING FOOD COOL AND SAFE

On layovers, the longer you stay in one spot, the more elaborate you can make your camp, but of prime importance is the safeguarding of food and keeping it fresh.

Opened cans of butter, surplus milk, vegetables, etc., can be kept cool in several ways. Lake or stream water is always available to make satisfactory coolers. Place the food in plastic bags; place the bags in a large watertight container; and partially submerge the container in shallow water, weighing it down with rocks.

CHOW TIME

Preparations and the eating of meals in the wilderness should be just as gracious and decorous as when eating at home. The cook should have the cooperation of all hands— supplying wood, tending a pot, setting out utensils, the bread, butter, etc., and anticipating other needs, so that all meal courses come out at the same time, after which the entire crew—including the cook—sit down to eat together, dining out in a setting of blue water, green islands, hazy shore lines, and gray rocks rising out of a carpet of moss more luxurious than any rug.

Part Three

LAUNCHING
THE EXPEDITION

7

Journey
to
Wilderness

YOU arrive at your last point of contact with civilization—whether at the end of the road, the place where you board a railway train or take off in a bush plane—the point where the crew brings together all the final strands of planning.

Your "Contact" Person

At or near your point of embarkation, you meet your contact person, with whom you've been corresponding since the early stages of planning for your trip, whether it be your first one or the latest of many. With him you recheck your plans, go over your lists, checking off each piece of equipment and gear, your supplies and grub, securing from an outfitter whatever fill-ins are required, resolving the problem of licenses and permits.

Once committed to the trail, there's no

turning back, and woe to him who forgot the first-aid kit, the extra paddle, the salt or sugar, or the waterproof matches.

Your contact man may be the outfitter, a game warden, a park official, the Hudson's Bay Post manager (if you embark from one such post in Canada), a guide, or some local canoe-trip enthusiast. He is the best source of the latest information on water conditions and the fishing action, on the insect problem and animal pests.

He will appraise your qualifications by looking over your personal condition, your garb, and your packsacks. To him you give (as well as to your family and a friend or two) your itinerary—your exact route and your destination. As a safety measure, the Royal Canadian Mounted Police are quick to assess a crew's experience and capability, and after learning the details of your trip—extent and duration, which Canadian officials require for wilderness areas—they will grant permission only if it is feasible.

Should a forest fire, a violent storm, or a flood occur, they'll know whether or not you are endangered and where to find you. Also, they know the dangers of wilderness travel— a broken limb, an attack of appendicitis, heart trouble, and other emergency situations—and that canoeists are far from conventional help.

Should a crew fail to show up at a proposed deadline, an extensive search is almost invariably touched off by the Royal Canadian Air Force. The cost, usually borne by the local province, is prodigious in both time and money, and officials take every precaution to prevent its need.

Trimming the Canoe

Ballast the canoe with the heavy gear (tent, wanigan, cooking hardware, etc.) below, and lighter gear on top—all in balance fore and aft and side to side. If necessary, place blankets or clothing between sharp-edged cargo and the hull.

Bind together the extra paddle, fishing rods, and ax, and wedge them beside the duffel, or at the bottom, so they won't fall overboard when the canoe lurches. Floatable items, such as most commercial food packets, need not be secured.

Leave no gear or equipment, no small bundles, hanging loose. Stow all in as few as possible packs, the advantages of which you'll recognize on the first portage. Cover all cargo amidships with a light tarpaulin, and lash its corners to the thwarts.

For proper trim, the bow is slightly higher than the stern, and the freeboard after the crew has boarded should be seven inches for smooth-water cruising, more for rough water on large lakes.

On way to layover days' adventures in Quetico Park, Ontario, the canoe has been properly trimmed.
ONTARIO DEPT. TOURISM & INFORMATION PHOTO

Expert canoeists using the slick water route through rocky obstructions in a Maine river.
OLD TOWN CANOE CO. PHOTO

The hull of the canoe, or any other water-craft, riding in the water, introduces complicating factors in maintaining the center of gravity—equilibrium—of the craft. The floating hull with its upward pressure resists passenger and cargo weight, which for stability must be centrally located, as low as possible, around the single point of balance. This is called the center of buoyancy in a floating craft. The proper center of buoyancy requires the hull shape and load weight to be in the same vertical plane as the center of gravity. A canoe thus stabilized will ride out the roughest water.

With the bow steadied on shore, the stern-man can actually walk along the gunwale to disembark without tipping a well-balanced canoe.

The Bowman's Role

The bowman is the tactical commander of a canoeing crew. It is his responsibility to keep the craft on a safe course, whether it be a rock-strewn river or open lake with high waves. In shallow, rock-strewn streams, it is advisable for the bowman to get out of the canoe and, by wading (wearing canvas shoes), pull it along, around boulders and other obstructions. His knowledge of paddle strokes should enable him to brake the canoe, to turn it sharply left or right, to back up or continue on a straight course—as conditions warrant.

The bowman calls upon many strokes (acting quickly in emergency situations of which

FLOTILLA OF CANOES POWERED BY OUTBOARD

Detail of towing bridle attached to stern thwart

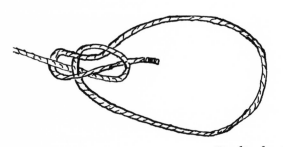

Bowline knot

Open Lake Travel

In heavy winds or quick squalls, the crew may choose the lee shore of large lakes and islands even though the route may be longer. Because rain, strong winds, high waves, and hail cause the majority of problems on lakes, whenever able to predict a storm, before crossing open water (it's not necessary to battle it), hole up and wait—storms subside (see Chapter 8).

Once committed, should you be caught in heavy, high-crested waves, instead of trying to drive straight through, quarter across them on a diagonal. The wind, in a tacking principle, actually helps the canoe forward with less danger of shipping water.

A paddler conserves muscle power by setting a course to make use of islands, headlands, and other natural windbreaks, and although the sheltered course may divert him from a more direct route, it requires less effort and sometimes can make the difference between crossing and not crossing.

Running downwind in a heavy sea, it is tempting to ride the waves without paddling. If you do, steerage (control) is lost, and there is danger of turning broadside to the surge of waves and becoming swamped. A pail tied to a rope and secured at the stern can be dragged (as a sea anchor) to slow the canoe in gale force winds.

The Kneeling Position

On a large body of water, in the event of a dangerous squall with high-crested waves,

the sternman is unaware), the quarter sweep, the pushover, pullover, diagonal draws, prying, and braking strokes, while the sternman makes proper adjustments. The sternman needs a bowman who can keep the canoe from cracking on the rocks or running aground on every sharp curve of meandering watercourses. Once the trip is underway, "eternal caution" is the word for the bowman.

Little wonder that during the fur-trading days of the 1700s and 1800s, the bowman was paid more than the stern paddler. Expert canoeists on wilderness trips select their bowman with great care.

turn the canoe into the wind, and kneel as low as possible in the canoe. The kneeling position is necessary in heavy seas. Paddlers wedge their knees against the sides of the canoe, brace the hips or the small of the back against the thwart or seat, and become a part of the craft, just as a cyclist becomes a part of his bike. The low position offers less resistance to the wind, expediting the paddling chore—an important factor in an all-day struggle against the wind.

The importance of kneeling in a canoe is best illustrated by the fact that the weight of a paddler sitting upon a seat or the always forbidden thwart is eight to twelve inches above the surface of the water, from which position, at a sudden lurch or bump, he can easily fall overboard.

Should it be necessary to continue paddling in breaking waves or in rain, check the cover over your cargo to make sure that the water is shed over the gunwales. Water that sloshes in the bottom of your canoe greatly affects your control of it. Periodically bail it out, and if possible beach the canoe and dump unwanted (water) ballast.

Should the bow, taking on water from big waves, tend to bury itself, both paddlers kneel and move toward each other if possible so that their weight falls amidships, abetting stability.

What If You Capsize?

The majority of canoeing accidents occur from capsizing. In the event of a capsize, stay with the swamped canoe. A canoe floats whether it's right side up, upside down, or punctured, has sufficient positive buoyancy to support the passenger capacity, and will support them inside even when the canoe is filled with water. It will support as many as a dozen persons holding onto the gunwales but not attempting to climb upon it.

Stay with a capsized canoe, for it can be more easily spotted from the shore, the air, or another canoe than individual canoeists can be.

The craft can be floated or pushed toward shallow water, or emptied in deep water if the shore is some distance away.

The Flip-over

Treading water easily, canoeists ease themselves below the surface and come up under the overturned canoe, one forward of the bow thwart, the other slightly aft of the stern thwart. Grasping the gunwales in a coordinated effort, on signal they heave the canoe (while vigorously treading water) straight up and give it a final flip so that the canoe falls upright on the surface. To prevent the canoe from being blown away, make the flip to the windward side.

The Shake-out

The canoeist also can shake out the water from a capsized canoe by swimming to a position amidships and grasping the gunwale with both hands, shoulder-width apart. Lower the near gunwale close to the top of the water, then thrust upward to start the water surging toward the opposite side. On the near-side gunwale, alternating a depression (pull down) with a thrust upward induces the water in the canoe to surge and to overflow the gunwales. Be prepared for the water to splash your face as it clears the near-side gunwale.

The timing is more important than strength, and a scissors kick helps. The rocking motion increases in vigor as the canoe empties.

After boarding (see below), hand paddle if necessary to retrieve paddles and other gear.

Canoe-over-Canoe Rescue

This is a lot simpler than it sounds, and involves little risk to the canoes and the canoeists who are using the gunwales for support while in the water awaiting rescue.

When rescuing a swamped canoe, paddle up to it so that:

1. The center of the rescuing canoe is perpendicular to the end of the swamped canoe.

2. Working from the center of their canoe, the rescuers grasp the deck and the stemband of the distressed canoe.

3. Gently lift the distressed canoe to start the water pouring toward the far end.

4. Pull the canoe up approximately two feet across (but not resting on) the gunwales of the rescuing canoe, to empty more water.

5. Roll the swamped canoe bottom side up, and pull it completely out of the water, supported, so that both canoes are gunwale to gunwale.

6. Flip the top canoe over, right side up, and feed it into the water in a hand-over-hand method.

7. Bring the rescued canoe alongside, and for re-entry of passengers, steady it by holding the gunwales of both canoes together.

In a windy open-lake situation, approach the capsized canoe downwind; and, in a strong current, approach upstream.

Re-Entry

Re-entering a canoe from the water is a useful skill each canoeist should acquire, whether or not in trouble. To board a swamped canoe, approach amidships and place both hands inside, on the bottom over the keel line (middle), and with a vigorous flutter kick, swim into the canoe. When the chin is over the far gunwale, twist the body and flop into a sitting position on the bottom of the canoe. Pivot around so that the legs are inside the canoe and the back supported by one of the thwarts. The arms may be extended sideways for balance, stability, and/or hand paddling.

When re-entering a dry canoe, the principles are essentially the same as above. Approaching amidships in a horizontal swimming position, reach across the canoe to the far-side gunwale, and with a vigorous kick and pull, bring the chest and thighs across the gunwale. A flip (or turn) of the body transfers the weight from the cross gunwale position to the bottom of the canoe, so that the canoeist lands in a sitting position. Bring the legs inside the canoe. This maneuver is simplified when a second crew member is in the water and steadies the craft for the re-entry.

Re-entering a canoe after a capsize and continuing forward progress in a wilderness situation generally refers to the unloaded canoe while the crew is fishing, exploring, prospecting, or visiting.

Salvage a Capsized Loaded Canoe

The loaded canoe, capsized or swamped, essentially develops into a salvage operation, and there should be little thought of re-entry and continuing a voyage. The first concern, naturally, is for the crew members, then for the retrieval of the essential cargo and the paddles.

Improvise a Sail

In a land of large lakes and anticipated foul weather, the seasoned traveler will do most of his paddling in the early morning before the wind blows (it seldom does before nine o'clock). Getting underway by 4 or 5 A.M., the canoeists can get a half-day's paddling before the storm makes further progress impossible.

With a wind at the crew's back while crossing a large lake or a straight stretch of river, rig an improvised sail. Lash a mast, cut in the woods, to the bow thwart. A top boom holds the sail (tarp, shirt, or poncho), while the bowman, who sits astride the mast on the bottom of the canoe, hand holds the lower corners of the sail. He can release the sail in case of sudden gusts of wind that endanger the craft because of the lack of a leeboard.

The sternman uses his paddle as a rudder.

The French Voyageurs, in a labor-saving strategem, pushed paddle shafts through shirt sleeves and held them aloft to catch the wind.

Lash Together Canoes

Lash two canoes together with the bows four feet apart and the sterns five to six feet apart, to prevent splash. Use three long poles, lashing the center pole to the middle thwarts, then the bow and stern thwarts. This rig makes it impossible to capsize either canoe.

Should you use an outboard motor, place it on the stern pole near one of the sternmen, for control and for more economical use of fuel. Two canoes lashed together with a suitable platform of boards are so stable that they can carry a small cement mixer!

During Fine Weather

All is well during fine weather, and there are long stretches of water to cruise with an outboard motor, and many purposeful things to be doing: trim finger and toenails, hone knives and axes, mend garments, sew buttons, rinse socks and handkerchiefs, repair fishing tackle, sun bathe in the nude, and arrange personal duffle. Above all, watch the course for tricky turns and the shore lines for landmarks—especially if the crew is going to backtrack the route many days later.

In Canada, one expects to see more magnificant conifers as he travels farther and farther northward into the hinterland. On our trip from Deer Lake to Sandy Lake in northern Ontario, we found this to be untrue—as it is in most regions above the fifty-second parallel. We traveled for days and for miles, and the water lost its blue color, changing to a clay-colored hue, and the trees diminished in size, eventually giving way to the low-growing muskeg that stretched endlessly from both shores of the rivers; a prelude to the tundra. In a land where the frost line was several inches below the spongy soil, campsites on solid ground were difficult to find.

The fishermen in the crew will discover many likely hot spots and be tempted to set up the rods and cast or troll, but do not weaken. Underway with a fully laden canoe, the group has but one objective—that of completing the day's route and making camp. The large fish have a way of striking when one is least prepared for them. Fishing is best done on layover days, or in the evening after the camp has been set up, dinner eaten, and the canoe and equipment secured (see Chapter 10).

8

Navigating the Water Trails

ON land and afloat, the canoeist orients himself with the memorization of map features: main bodies of water (lakes); the general course of a river, its source and destination; declivity in the land, ridges, hills, and the lowlands too.

Study the map symbols to impress upon your mind these features.

Constantly refer to the map with a compass, a necessary adjunct to the map. A compass doesn't show the way; it's a direction instrument denoting north, and from that one constant, you figure your position and your direction.

Use your compass, reading it constantly, and watch the sun as a double check, as the presence of metal can swing the compass needle to an improper reading.

Declination of Compass

As most wilderness canoe waters are located within the northern part of the hemisphere, be sure the crew understands the declination of the compass needle. The geographic North Pole is the true north, but the compass needle points to the magnetic north pole, which in varying degree is a section of far northern Canada—north of Hudson Bay. The two poles are not the same.

Because the compass needle points to the north magnetic pole, for a specific reading (direction) the declination must be taken into account. The closer to the North Pole a canoeist navigates, the greater is the degree of compass error from true north. Most maps

61

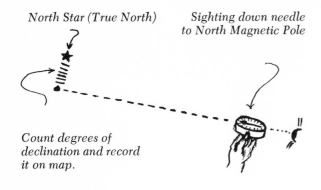

North Star (True North)   *Sighting down needle to North Magnetic Pole*

Count degrees of declination and record it on map.

DETERMINING DECLINATION OF COMPASS

include a diagram indicating the amount of declination for the region. For true orientation, you must note the degree of correction.

Have faith in your compass. A sense of direction is not the instinctive "gift" many outdoorsmen claim to possess. A number of experiments indicate that man, with no known landmarks available, will travel in a complete circle—left to right, or right to left: therefore, every crew member of the wilderness canoe should have both a compass and a map, and refer often to both. When a question arises, check one another's opinion.

Many tricky outlets from large lakes, and rivers with many tributaries, must be hit on the button to avoid getting lost and to save time and energy. Also, when navigating around an island-studded lake, it is necessary

Portage on the Sand River, after being dropped off the Algoma Central Railroad.
ONTARIO DEPT. TOURIST & INFORMATION PHOTO

to stay on course by making adjustments for the declination of compass.

Portaging

Cruising along, the crew should be constantly on the lookout for turbulent waters by observation and careful reference to the map. Study the elevation and contour symbols for your location. The difference of elevation in land from one point to another, within a short distance, indicates a drop of water in the form of falls or rapids. Portaging on land offers no problem in water turbulence. A height of land between lakes makes necessary a hump-back portage where the watershed on the far side will be reversed (flow away) from the waterway you left.

On a river course, it is usually the bowman who sights rough water, and the signal to portage must be given in ample time. Sometimes the decision for taking out or shooting the rapids must be anticipated far in advance. More often than not, that decision should be to portage around the turbulence. "After all, no one ever drowned on a portage," is an old wilderness saying.

It is wise to take out as soon as one hears the rumble of water, or sees the rising spray. As soon as possible, determine the take-out side. The portage path, no matter where, how long, or why there, was made by canoeists who sought the shortest and the easiest way between lakes or around turbulences.

The Cree Indians of northern Ontario, Canada, place a long pole on the shore of a lake to indicate an outlet, or on the riverbank to indicate the take-out side. Sometimes on little traveled portages, the trail will be overgrown with weeds, and it is necessary to probe with the feet to find it. The portage trail may not be the most direct, but once traversing it, you find it the easiest and most expeditious route.

Don't attempt to portage a canoe right side up with duffel inside. If either of the carriers slip, you are almost certain to end up with a hole in the canoe from the boulders or stumps that line the path. Long portages call for a rest halfway across. Many portages have canoe rests—two vertical posts with a horizontal member on top. You lean the canoe against these, and step out from under and take a break. Then you won't have to lift it

After canoes have been carried to a safe place, the packs are carried first on portage.
DEPT. OF INDUSTRY & COMMERCE, REGINA, SASKATCHEWAN

At the end of a portage in De La-Vérendrye Park.
PROVINCE OF QUEBEC FILM BUREAU PHOTO

when you start again. In the absence of canoe rests, a forked or branched tree of suitable height can be used.

In making unfamiliar portages, carry the lighter, less bulky gear first; note the character of the trail: windfalls, obstructing branches, slippery logs or roots, and muddy places. Improve the trail wherever possible before portaging the canoe. It is more efficient to carry loads short distances and to rest frequently while walking back for another load on long portages.

Outlets at the end of lakes are generally in cattail-filled, reedy, or marshy areas, completely screening out the portage path. Many times it is possible to discover the meandering outlet, and pull the canoe through instead of portaging.

The dotted line on maps indicating portages are designated in chains, approximately: 1 chain = 66 feet.

Portages are necessary in a wilderness trip, but often they prompt caustic remarks. A veteran canoeist once said, "There are two types of language used on a trip—one is the talk around the campfire, the other is reserved for portages." Once, when I asked a canoeist who was finishing a portage, "Was it an easy one?" dropping his packsack with a thud and wiping his brow, he replied, "There are no easy portages."

The attitude toward portaging reflects the caliber of the crew members. They should accept the labor as a part of the price of enjoying the hinterland. After all, many less adventurous souls are screened out by difficult portages. The change of pace from long cruises, using different muscles and enjoying the scenery through the woods, or watching the break in water as it cascades and tumbles down a narrow incline, foams and gentles in the pool below, are treasures along the way.

It is best to load or unload a canoe while it is parallel to the shore and floating free. If necessary, one crew member wades alongside and transfers the cargo in or out of the canoe. There's no hurry on portages, and frequent stops for rest should be taken if needed. There should always be time for photography and fishing. The pools below water turbulence are where the walleyes congregate, and often it is possible to catch, filet, and pack them for the evening meal.

Tracking a Canoe

Tracking is a procedure for pulling a canoe upstream, and is used when the water is too fast and too turbulent for successful upstream paddling. Secure long line (painter) of about fifty feet to the bow ring or bow thwart, tie another to the stern thwart. One crew member can work both lines, or two canoeists, one on each line, pull the canoe along in deep water, away from shore obstructions, while walking along the bank or wading in shallow water. Releasing the bow line and pulling on the stern line drives the canoe farther out into the river: pulling the bow line and releasing the stern line will bring the canoe toward the trackers (shoreward).

Keep the canoe headed upstream by adjusting the relative lengths and tension on the two lines.

Another method is to use the bow line only, while a second crew member keeps the canoe offshore with a long pole. Walk cautiously, and constantly check your footing and the reaction of the canoe.

On the first trip over a portage trail, take a light pack to reconnoiter the path for difficulty and obstacles before carrying across the canoe.
COURTESY COLORADO OUTDOOR SPORTS CORP.

Lining a Canoe

Lining is a matter of guiding the canoe downstream (the opposite of tracking) with a long line, over difficult water too dangerous to run. One or two canoeists control the canoe's position and progress as in tracking. The constant alignment of the canoe with the current is important.

CAUTION: In lining and in tracking, control is the watchword. Never allow the canoe to come broadside of the current. Check and double check the tie on the rope, making certain that the line is strong, as the current places great strain on the towing lines.

Poling

Professional canoeists — Indians, trappers, prospectors, and others—use the setting pole for quick water in shallow or rocky streams up to three feet in depth. The upright stance of the poler, with his forward leg pressed against the thwart, feet apart and toed in, gives constant control to the canoe as he executes the thrust of the pole.

Some polers, sweeping the pole forward in quick thrusts against the bottom, to maintain better balance, never remove the pole from the water. When using this method, the pole is almost constantly near the bottom and is set for any emergency.

The other method is to thrust the pole to the bottom and push backward, climbing the pole hand-over-hand. The recovery is made by lifting the pole completely out of the water.

In downstream travel, use the pole to snub or to break the momentum. There is sustained control for stopping, changing direction, and for threading through a maze of boulders. In upstream travel, the poler must keep the bow headed into the current. Plotting the course by selecting water with the least force (usually at the edges of a stream), or using a calm eddy, crossing and recrossing the main current to best advantage, are all factors that must be experienced rather than read about.

The bow of the canoe, whether going up or downstream, should be trimmed low to abet alignment. The bowman, using a paddle in conventional strokes, and the sternman, using the pole, make an efficient combination.

Sometimes the most effective portage is in the middle of a river, when the rock formation is favorable.
OLD TOWN CANOE CO. PHOTO

In shooting rapids, the combination of poling and paddling is used. OLD TOWN CANOE CO. PHOTO

Improvise a Pole

Ash, maple, or spruce, of about an inch and a quarter in diameter, ten to twelve feet long, make ideal poles. Poles should be peeled and trimmed of knobs for hand comfort and safety. Should a lot of poling be in the trip plan, buy a steel shoe (spiked tip), and nail it to the pole. Carry the steel shoe as equipment, even though the pole can be discarded after use.

BECOME WEATHERWISE

There's no daily weather report for the wilderness canoeist: he must be his own meteorologist. As local observations determine local weather, personal observations without instrumentation can lead with surprising accuracy to forecasts of what is going to happen within the next few hours, perhaps the next twenty-four. The cosmic pulse of weather is tuned to rhythm, as are light, heat, and sound waves. Weather cycles have definite patterns

—measured in centuries. They are like the waves of the sea, some higher than others, but following a pattern, a scheme of repetition, so that between every two high waves there are repeated series of smaller ones. "Every cloud has a silver lining," is not without logic.

In time, anyone can become weatherwise. Certain broad principles can be acquired by reading books, but the best learning comes from living outdoors with the weather—watching its components, recording its signs.

Develop the habit of studying the sky and its clouds, the temperature, wind, and humidity, and take note of the phenomena which accompany and follow their various combinations.

The making of weather is readily discernible, especially in the plainest sign of all—the clouds. Every morning, and throughout the day, the outdoorsman watches the clouds of his bit of sky.

CUMULUS CLOUDS, lofty, white, and puffy, dome-shaped on top, the base generally horizontal, usually indicate fair weather. When a cumulus cloud becomes dark underneath as

Heavy descending clouds indicate time to get off water and prepare for a blow at Superior-Quetico, Minnesota.
JOHN W. MALO PHOTO

it approaches, rain is possible and should the underside become pink or coppery, expect the worst, get to shore, pitch the tent, and secure all gear.

CIRRUS CLOUDS, thin, high wisps, feather-like and delicate in body, with clouds moving under them in different directions, indicate unpleasant weather ahead.

CUMULONIMBUS CLOUDS (thunderheads), in line, in the form of mountains, on the western or northwestern horizon, growing larger and coming fast, soon will bring accompanying lightning and thunder. Count the seconds after a flash of lightning until you hear thunder: a five-second interval indicates that the storm is approximately a mile away.

No matter how large, high clouds generally indicate fair weather, but keep an eye on them. Should they descend, rain may fall.

When clouds lose their shape, run together, become scrambled, expect immediate rain and possibly thundershowers. After they've expended their moisture, they seem to form again into definite shape—indicating the rain has ended.

WIND DIRECTION is another aid to canoe-country weather prediction. The prevailing wind keeps leaves on trees and shrubs in an orderly pattern; but when the leaves are ruffled by the wind, exposing their undersides, a changing wind is indicated and bears watching.

NORTH AND EAST WINDS often bring cold and rain. The summer northeaster is generally protracted, with rain lasting three or four days.

SOUTH AND SOUTHEAST WINDS often signify the coming of rain within the day. The summer southeaster represents a wet, windy condition with velocity of gale-like proportions. The southwest, west, and northwest winds are the fairest of all for the canoeist.

Weather is directly tied with wind conditions. The canoeist can go about his cooking, camping, and paddling in the rain, heat, or cold even in some discomfort; but gale force winds whipping up the water (he may have paddled before) can infringe upon the proposed route and schedule, for the business of the canoeist is to travel a water route and not get swamped.

The same wind over land and over water is more violent, and the turbulence greater, over the water. Nothing can instill a greater feeling of helplessness than a storm on an open lake —its onset, fury and force beyond comprehension—and the canoeist must respect it as he respects the force and the volume of the powerful rushing water on a rock-strewn rapid in a stream.

Late one afternoon, on a wilderness trip, Hal Emiley, Bob Kuehnert, and I kept tabs on an approaching storm over Barton Lake, decided against going ashore, and headed for a known, more desirable campsite farther along. We paddled in a race with the coming fury. We almost didn't make it: the storm hit and whipped the water into whitecaps, so that we had difficulty making shore just forty feet away. Had we been but a few feet farther lakeward, we couldn't have paddled against the wind and would have been blown across the several-mile-wide lake.

We made our second mistake, when, in the frenzy of pitching our tent in a gale and rain, we placed it over a mossy bed. Securing our gear under the canoe, we ate a cold dinner in the tent. All night long the moss (without a root system), like a sponge, absorbed the water surrounding it, and we slept on the watery mattress under our drop cloth. It gurgled and swished every time we turned in our sleeping bags.

MORAL: Respect weather signs and pitch camp early!

Thunderstorms

Summer, supposedly, is the calm time of the year: the sun takes over, warms the earth and stabilizes the weather; but the sun has competition that affects weather. Large bodies of water are almost icy cold, and icebergs drift southward from the Arctic Circle. The warm air from land masses rises and drifts away at the upper levels to settle perhaps over the cold water of the Great Lakes, Hudson Bay, and the Labrador Current. More warm air is drawn from the Gulf of Mexico and the Gulf Stream. When the cool air from the north and northeast creeps under and over the warm, humid air, thunderstorms are born and copious rain may fall for a day or days.

Lightning is the jagged flash of light in the sky from one cloud to another, or from a cloud to earth, caused by the discharge of atmospheric electricity. The positive and negative charges accumulate until they have enough force to leap and unite with opposite charges in an unpredictable pattern; sometimes a single flash, other times, several discharges may shoot along the same path, again and again.

The lightning bolt that passes from cloud to earth is the most dangerous to the outdoorsman. The lightning travels from a cloud to the earth object, generally the one nearest to it: i.e., a tall tree, church steeple, hill, or mountain: therefore, do not stand near any object that draws lightning. Don't stay in the middle of an open body of water; don't expose yourself upright atop a hill.

The bottom of a ravine or gully is reasonably safe. That's why a tent should never be pitched on the highest point of land or under the tallest trees. Should you become trapped on a high elevation, though you'll get soaked, the safest place during a thunderstorm is at some distance from trees and lofty objects.

Lightning travels along the line of least resistance, but it has been known inexplicably to hit other and lower objects in our hemisphere.

Lightning flashes in the west or northwest mean that the storm is coming your way. Storms in the south and the east will go past your campsite.

Some recorded weather maxims are based on scientific fact and date back to the clay tablets of Babylonia. Select the factual maxims and forget the unproved ones: for instance, since the early years of A.D., this has survived: "Evening red and morning gray, help the traveler on his way: evening gray and morning red, bring down rain upon his head."

The rising sun shining red through fogless atmosphere and the lit-up undersurface of clouds indicate dry weather to the east, but thickening clouds and rain where you are. The best rising sun is one ascending through a hazy, cloudy, or foggy horizon.

Sailors (and canoeists) take warning when there's a rainbow in the morning. "The rainbow at night is the canoeist's delight."

"Rain before seven will usually clear before eleven."

A sky color of deep blue, even when seen through clouds, indicates fair weather; while a glowing whiteness to the sky indicates a coming storm.

Sun dogs are the halos around both the sun and the moon. The large circles or parts of circles, occurring after fine weather, indicate a change.

"When the grass is dry at morning's light, look for rain before the night."

The higher the clouds, the finer the weather.

Should you plan an early take-off and a radiation fog shrouds the land and water, go ahead; the fog is usually of short duration and is dissipated as the rising sun heats the earth.

A heavy dew on the grass at night or in early morning is a good indication of a clear day ahead. It forms only when there's a lack of moisture in the air and the skies are clear.

High barometric pressure causes the smoke from your campfire to rise straight up and waterfowl to fly high in the absence of wind —indicating good weather.

When there is moisture in the air, the barometric pressure is low, which causes the smoke from your campfire to flatten out and travel along the ground, and waterfowl to fly low or to perch—indicating foul weather.

There's the age-old aching of rheumatic joints representing a coming change in weather.

One fairly reliable rule is when the onset of gathering clouds is rapid and rain comes suddenly, it will probably clear up soon. Should the period of cloud build-up be long and it begins to rain, chances are that it will be a several-hour rain.

SUMMARY: STORMY WEATHER is indicated by: a red sunrise, no morning dew, muggy and sticky atmosphere, any wind from the southeast or east, a rising temperature and a falling barometer; cricket and other insect sounds seeming extra loud; dark clouds massing on the western horizon; clouds moving at various heights in different directions; clouds dropping lower and lower; and a gray or dull sunset.

FAIR WEATHER is indicated by: misty, foggy sunrise, heavy morning dew on the grass, foggy morning conditions, a falling temperature and a rising barometer, campfire smoke rising straight up, spiders spinning webs, cloudless skies, high, stationary, isolated clouds, moderate winds from the west or the northwest, and a red sunset.

Even with instruments, weather forecasting can be an inexact science; but making your own weather reports from cloud behavior, haze, visibility, and sensing changes in temperature, humidity, and wind, can enable the canoeing party to come through safely and happily.

9

Pitching Camp

To assure a safe and secure campsite experience and to avoid frenzied, last-minute setup, cooking, dishwashing, and securing of gear by flashlight, the knowledgeable wilderness canoeists begin their search for a campsite long before sunset.

HOW LONG TO SUNSET?

A simple woodsman's trick, without the use of a watch, is to extend the arms toward the sun, turn fingers inward at right angles to the wrist. The little finger of one hand rests on the pointer (index) finger of the other, with thumbs at right angles to the index fingers. Compute fifteen minutes for each finger between the horizon and the lower edge of the sun. This gives approximate sunset time; and there'll be more minutes of twilight before darkness sets in.

There may be times in the wilderness experience that even without a watch, the crew can estimate the proper time to keep a bush plane appointment, to meet a railway train at some wilderness siding, or to accomplish some other end. The time can be computed from the Sunrise Time chart, for various latitudes, and sunset from the Sunset Time chart.

CAUTIOUS CAMPSITE CONSIDERATIONS

Never camp on a beach, as sand has a way of sifting into shoes, clothing, sleeping bags, utensils, fishing reels, cameras, and food.

Check for a supply of dry firewood and a safe place for the cooking fire—and campfire —bare soil, rock, or sand.

Select a campsite on the sheltered side of a point, cove, riverbank, or an island.

73

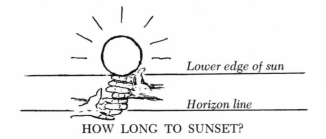

Lower edge of sun

Horizon line

HOW LONG TO SUNSET?

To determine the amount of time to sunset, without a watch, extend arms toward the sun and turn fingers inward at right angles to the wrist. Compute 15 minutes for each finger between sun and horizon. The example above indicates 90 minutes.

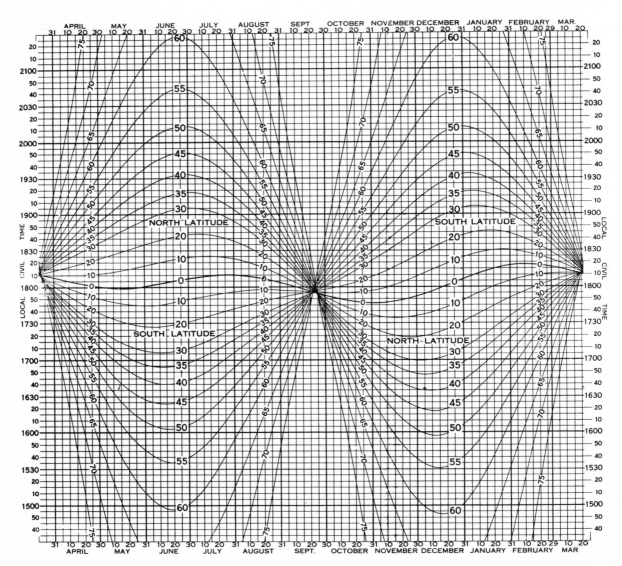

SUNSET DIAGRAM

EXAMPLE

What is sunrise time in latitude 40 degrees N, longitude 77 degrees W, July 10?

Enter at bottom for July 10 and move vertically up to 40 degrees on the North Latitude curve.

Move horizontally left, and read Local Civil Time of 0430 (4:30 A.M.).

Note: Your longitude does not affect the Local Civil Time of sunrise.

These diagrams portray graphically for any year the times of rising and setting of the sun for latitudes up to 75 degrees, north and south. For high latitudes, not included on the diagrams, twilight or half light will usually be found throughout the summer nights.

The scales at the top and bottom of the page mark the date for every five days, while the vertical

scales divide the Local Civil Time into five-minute intervals. The latitudes appear on the curves. For values between the plotted values, interpolate by eye. This may be done to one day of time, to approximately one degree of latitude and to one minute of Local Civil Time. Accuracy of the diagrams is to within one or two minutes.

INSTRUCTIONS FOR USE

1. *Enter the top or bottom scale with the proper date.*
2. *Move vertically down or up to curve for the observer's latitude.*
3. *Move horizontally to the right or left and read Local Civil Time on the vertical scales at the side.*

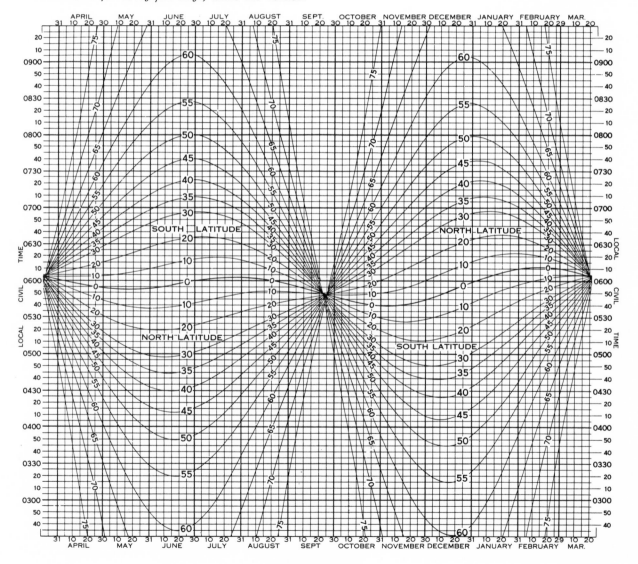

SUNRISE   DIAGRAM

FROM *The Log*, AN EXPLORERS JOURNAL, WINTER 1970, USED BY PERMISSION.

If your contact person has indicated that it is "a bad year for bears," perhaps a small island or a narrow peninsula would be the best campsite.

Islands are generally preferred locales because the chances of starting an extensive forest fire are fewer and they have fewer insects.

One general rule is to pitch your tent in the open, away from both tall trees and brush, because of lightning, falling branches, ventilation, and insects.

When the flies and mosquitoes (mosquitoes are predictable, preferring shade to sunlight and seeming to be attracted to light-colored clothing) are thick, select the most exposed, wind-swept site available.

Within the exposed, wind-swept site there lies a paradox. Should a strong wind or rainstorm threaten your exposed tent, a setting among poplar or birch tree stands would be the better place to pitch—and take your chances with the "bug" problem.

Prevailing Winds

Your first and fundamental consideration is the prevailing wind, for it determines the position in which you pitch your tent. Unpredictable rains and squalls usually come from the south, the southeast, and/or from the west: therefore, the opening of the tent always should face a northerly direction, so that storms coming up during the night will not blow it down before you can close and secure your tent.

At all times during the day, keep the tent closed, as strong winds can enter an open tent and rip your only shelter—even beyond repair.

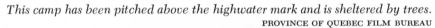

This camp has been pitched above the highwater mark and is sheltered by trees.
PROVINCE OF QUEBEC FILM BUREAU

Campsite Drainage

Drainage is important. Regardless of weather forecasts, plan as if it were going to rain like fury during the trip and especially, unexpectedly, at night. If so, will you be sleeping in or over running water?

To check the drainage pattern of the area, look for any debris that has been washed down during former rains.

On hilly terrain, which is usual in most wilderness areas, ditching the two high sides of the tent should provide adequate drainage for it.

An Ideal Campsite

1. Proper drainage;
2. Tall trees on the west and on the southwest of the tent site;
3. Adequate air circulation;
4. Ample wood for fires (campfire and cooking);
5. Huge boulders to serve as tables and seats;
6. A long, broad view of the lake or the river;
7. Good fishing waters if your party includes fishing as one of their activities.

There is always some trial and error in campsite selection, as "absolutes" don't exist. It should be heartening to know that the perfect wilderness campsite has never been discovered, but many of them are as near perfect as you could arrange, and one hopes for the best.

SECURING CANOES AND PADDLES

The campsite determined, never leave a canoe water-borne, tethered, or pulled halfway out of the water. The action of the wind and the waves pounding the canoe against rocks or branches causes damage; and should your canoe come loose, it could float away, irretrievably.

Always, immediately lift (don't drag) the canoe completely onto the shore and turn it over. If the landing site is rocky, place down boughs or poles to protect the canoe before hauling it up from shore. Select a locale where a high wind won't roll the canoe against a boulder or into the water. Articles not needed when sleeping may be stowed under it during the night.

Get into the habit of placing paddles upright in a bush or against a tree. Have you ever heard of anyone stepping on a paddle that was in an upright position? The thin blade of the paddle is easily split and the shaft easily broken. Never lay paddles on the ground or on a sandy beach where they can be stepped upon and broken. Never leave a paddle in the hot sun where the heat will warp it. Although I have never personally known of an occasion requiring the remedying of a badly warped paddle, I've heard of such and am acquainted with the remedial measure the Indians use—burying the paddle in the mud for several days (on a layover).

Your night's sleep will be more sound knowing you've taken these canoe and paddle precautions.

PITCH THE TENT PROMPTLY

Once the campsite has been reached, do not dally: set up the tent(s) immediately after carrying cargo and canoe(s) to safety. Conversely, when breaking camp, take down the tent last. The snugness of a pitched tent, with canoe and gear secured, is preferred, regardless of weather, and is especially appreciated in inclement weather.

Inverted canoes above highwater mark on the Delta River in Alaska.
U.S. DEPT. OF THE INTERIOR: BUREAU OF LAND MANAGEMENT

SAFE STORAGE OF PADDLES AT CAMPSITE

DRINKING WATER

Obviously, the quantity of water in the wilderness is adequate. The vital question is, "What is the QUALITY of the drinking and cooking water?

Most wilderness streams and lakes purify themselves, and their water is more pure and palatable than water from a city tap. The quality of water out in the lake, pulled up by a bucket tied to a rope to eliminate surface floating particles, is generally more clear and of more desirable quality. Spring water bubbling out of a sand declivity in wilderness areas is almost invariably safe to drink without treatment.

But, appearances can be deceptive. The clearest spring or stream can be contaminated. If the water you consume at the campsite is not pure and safe, your trip will be spoiled; by drinking water contaminated by germs or viruses of such contagious diseases as typhoid and dysentery, your health can be seriously impaired and perhaps permanently damaged.

A single cabin, a well-used campsite, or a cluster of dwellings situated near the water can create an unsafe situation. Sewage from humans generally finds its way into the nearest watercourse, and running water can carry dangerous germs great distances. Should your campsite area be well-traveled or down river from a concentration of habitations, or if for any reason there is the slightest doubt of its purity, the water must be treated.

Filtering water through sand or charcoal are inadequate methods of purification, for those agents merely strain out cloudy sediment, making the water clear and eye-appealing without removing dangerous germs or viruses.

Since it is impossible to test impure water except with laboratory equipment, there are two simple precautions the canoeist can take to ensure a safe water supply for both cooking and drinking at the campsite and when cruising: first, always boil the water for at least ten minutes; and, second, treat the water with recommended chemicals.

Boiled water loses some of its taste, but you can remedy that by adding a small quantity of powdered lemon juice or a pinch of salt. Aerate the cooled boiled water by pouring it back and forth from one sterilized vessel to another. The one disadvantage of sterilizing

With the canoe safely secured, the first order of business is pitching the tent, then setting out the sleeping and cooking area.
COURTESY COLORADO OUTDOOR SPORTS CORP.

Tripod for tepee, miner's, or pyramid tent

Four poles for umbrella tent

Rope ridge for pitching a tent in clearings

Ridge pole and two shear poles for emergency tarp tent

Ridge line adjustable by use of two shear poles

Shear poles with overhead and wall poles

RE-ENFORCEMENT FOR A SAGGING TENT

water by boiling is that the supply must be boiled well ahead of drinking time to cool sufficiently. Take advantage of a cooking fire or the evening campfire to boil the water and then store it covered for future use.

For campers, probably the most convenient water purification method is the use of especially prepared tablets. Add two Halzone tablets (a commercial product) to a quart of water and allow it to stand for thirty minutes: or, add two drops of tincture of iodine to each quart of water.

Chloride of lime, a powerful chemical that you use for latrine disinfectant, can be used for purifying water. The general measurements are: one teaspoon of chloride of lime added to a gallon of water makes a powerful treating solution. Do NOT use that solution for cooking or laundry, and do NOT drink it. Add only one part of the solution to each hundred parts of water. Before using the treated water, allow thirty minutes for purifying action.

CAMP SANITATION

An effective sanitation operation for the disposal of garbage, grease, and human wastes is of utmost importance to healthy, safe, and high-quality outdoor living.

Garbage and Grease Disposal

To prevent your garbage dump from becoming a restaurant for undesirable animals, burn or bury all garbage. Even though within the wilderness pack there is a minimum of tin containers, after use they should be burned out, then flattened and buried under at least three inches of covering soil. Should your camping area receive much use, it is advisable to tote out empty aluminum cans, glass,

and unburnable plastic containers, as the soil has an absorption-toleration level.

Use the grease pit to dispose of liquid wastes, dishwater, and other liquid disposables. Dig a hole downslope of the kitchen area, and line it with small stones or gravel to permit the water to filter through it while the grease sticks to the pebbly surfaces. Later, burn the solidified grease with a quick-burning fire of dry grass, sticks, or paper.

NOTE: Preserve in cans the straight grease from bacon, as on a wilderness trip there seems always to be a shortage of frying fats—especially when cooking fish.

Latrines

Although it is rare to find a latrine on a wilderness trail, use it when provided. The self-devised latrine is a must for wilderness travelers. Its location should be downhill from camp—at least 100 feet away (if possible). For one- or two-night campsite stands, the cat-hole type is adequate. Simply dig a hole, as a cat does, and after use, cover with soil.

Should there be no natural screen of bushes or brush, whatever the length of layover, build one of brush, canvas, or plastic sheeting. Even cats dislike being observed when they use a hole.

For layovers, or when campers of both sexes are in the group, a more efficient or elaborate latrine is necessary: a horizontal log, a pile of soil from the trench excavation, and a shovel left near the latrine are necessities. After use, sprinkle chloride of lime or wood ashes you've saved from the campfires to counteract odor, to keep away flies, and to hasten decomposition. Putting a match to used toilet paper reduces it to an ash, discourages flies, and prevents it from blowing away before covering it with soil.

The flat, folding type of toilet tissue, such as used in public restroom dispensers, is best. Each morning, each camper places a supply of tissue in shirt or pants pockets; when needed during the day, there's no rummaging around for a supply. The tissues also can be used for wiping camera lenses, binoculars, and sunglasses.

Nearby, a container of water, a basin, and a bar of soap help maintain proper sanitation standards. All hand-washing, laundering, and dishwashing should be done in a wash pan (not in a stream or lake), with treated water (see above), and the used water disposed of where it cannot get into the water supply before it filters through the ground. Why not dig a hole or horizontal trench for water disposal?

Observing simple rules of sanitation protects not only your crew, but also those who follow, just as you have to count on those who precede you on the trail to observe the same high sanitary standards.

Before you leave camp, cover the grease and garbage pits, the latrine and hand-washing water pit with soil. Mark each with an upright stick to apprise the next group of campers of their location. Leave your campsite the way you should like to find it.

Above all, remember, stack some firewood for the next party, just as you hope to find a supply at your next campsite.

Axmanship

In the hands of an enthusiastic, but unskilled camper, the ax probably is the most dangerous piece of equipment in camp. Obviously, the wilderness campsite is no place to practice extensive ax work: leave that to the most skilled and experienced camper.

Somewhere between the hatchet with a nail puller and a double-bitted, tree-felling ax is the ideal tripping ax. Certain types are popular in various locales, but for the canoeist to eliminate the problem of selection from the many types, there are a few broad guiding principles.

The wilderness ax, used mainly in the summer, can be a light model, single-bitted ax. The dividing line between light and heavy axes seems to be three and a half pounds: those weighing more are considered heavy. Some canoeists think it is better to be over-axed (have heavier model) than under-axed: others claim that the light one can cut an evening's supply of wood with half the effort.

When weight is a consideration on a wilderness canoe-camping trip, the light tool, the tripping ax with a single bit, which doubles as a pounding maul for stakes and cooking poles, hammering out dents in pots, pans, and a metal canoe, is recommended. The Hudson Bay pattern, with a head weight of one and three-quarter pounds and a twenty-four-inch

For sharpening your ax, use a 7- to 8-inch flat or mill file, using coarse side first, then fine side. Stroke only one way.

Hone in a circular motion with carborundum or oil-stone to remove the burr left by the filing process.

SHARPENING YOUR AX

In lopping off branches, work from the trunk to the crown, standing on one side of the trunk and cutting the branches from the opposite side.

The crotch of a log, firmly set on the ground, makes a firm splitting cradle.

To chop a log, cut one "v" halfway through, turn it and cut a similar "v" to meet the first. Chop alternately right and left to send the chips flying.

Splitting kindling on a stump, chopping block, or log.

Cut small branch diameters at an angle on a stump or firm log. To prevent sticks from flying, wedge one end under a rock or log.

The tent stake or pole is sharpened on four sides to a point for better penetration.

Use side of ax for all hammering chores.

When it is not being used, or sheathed, imbed the ax in a log or stump.

AXMANSHIP

handle, will do practically the same work as a full-sized ax. When properly used, it's capable of bringing down some pretty good-sized trees, and when sheathed is easy to stow and to carry.

The short-handled ax for chopping or splitting wood is particularly dangerous, as the blade is frequently traveling toward the leg or foot. Kneeling down when chopping and splitting wood gives better leverage and helps avoid that danger.

At all times the handle should be kept tight (by soaking in water or driving in a wedge), and the blade sharp. Both should be checked daily, for an ax with a blade that won't bite or a head that needlessly keeps slipping or flying off is dangerous. Sharpen the ax by first thinning it down with a mill file, drawing the file down against the edge of the blade to remove burrs and nicks. Then stroke the edge with the coarse side of a hone, and finish off with the smooth side, using a circular motion. Frequently, the ax is a pet tool, and little wonder that the owner is reluctant to lend it to any or all members of the crew.

Felling a tree is rarely justified today (hence is not discussed in this book), nor is it legal, even in most back country. Practically all wood needs can be scouted locally from fallen or dead trees.

When chopping, always check the back-swing area for obstructions; if branches or vines are within striking distance, particularly above or beside you, first top them off. Make certain that your footing is good. Use smooth rhythmic strokes, without too much force.

Before swinging, measure the distance by holding the ax edge where the cut is to be, and move yourself either closer or away as needed (very much as a golfer addresses the ball). Your arms should not be stretched: if they are, you're too far away.

The proper grip for chopping is to hold the handle with the left hand, about two inches from the end, while the right hand grips the handle about three-quarters of the way toward the head. From this position, bring the ax up so that the left arm is across the chest and the right hand is up about eight inches from the right ear. The ax head then travels in an arc to the target. The ax comes down with a natural swinging motion, the right hand sliding down the handle as the ax descends.

On heavy wood, the cutting angle is important, and a forty-five degree V groove is most efficient. This angle-cutting, alternately left and right, pries out the chips to keep the notch open. A general rule for efficient cutting through a heavy log is to make the V notch (kerf) as broad as the diameter. The cut is not made on top of the log, but on the far side, for better ax stroke leverage and for safety.

When lopping branches from a fallen tree, stand on the far side (the trunk between you and the branch) and cut up-branch for better bite and safety from a deflecting ax head.

It takes a long time to acquire skill in ax-manship. A few other principles include:

1. Carry the ax over your shoulder with the blade pointing outward—away from the head.

2. Slick gloves and restrictive clothes while chopping impair safety and efficiency.

3. Never stick the ax into a tree overhead, where it may fall out, endangering anyone underneath.

4. It's all right to leave a single bit ax stuck firmly in a chopping block or a log, but never leave it there overnight.

5. Keep the ax out of the sun.

6. Lay the sheathed ax flat in the tent to protect it from dampness and from handle-chewing porcupines.

7. Periodically, oil the sheath and smear a bit of bacon grease or fat on the cutting edge of the ax to prevent rusting.

Folding Saws

In view of the inherent dangers of the ax, the folding saw, which quickly rips through firewood, looms large in the eyes of a crew leader because it is more efficient for all small diameter cutting and the inexperienced camper can use it without peril to life or limb. The folding saw for back-packing is a version of the bow saw or "Swedish Fiddle," and it is ideally suited for many jobs in camp.

Comfort at the Campsite

Man is adaptable to many climes; he can live in extremes of temperature and yet thrive: in fact, 200 degrees separate the coldest from the hottest inhabited spots on earth. The chief single factor in human comfort is the rate at which heat is lost by the body, according to Dr. Leonard Hill, British scientist.

Exercise generates heat that warms the body, and ultimately that heat escapes into surrounding space, making the person comfortable. Should the heat escape be not sufficient (as when a person is wearing airtight rain gear), discomfort follows. Hot, humid air also prevents the body heat from being lost fast enough, also causing discomfort.

Loose-knit wear, permitting evaporation of perspiration in hot weather and offering warmed cells (insulation of air) next to the body in cold weather, is ideal. A windbreaker over wool represents the same principle, requiring no heavy apparel. Ideal garments for day and night wear, then, permit evaporation in hot weather and retain heat in cold-weather situations. (See Chapter 14 for information on the wind-chill factor.)

Sleeping Gear Care

All sleeping gear requires constant vigilance along the trail and at the campsite, for at all times it MUST BE KEPT DRY. A cold, damp, or uneven bed does not afford the required rest. The wilderness canoeist can take a lot of punishment during the day, but needs a good night's sleep to start afresh in the morning.

To encourage comfortable sleep further, if you use a pillow, fill a pillow case with an extra shirt, socks, pine needles, grass, or sweater. Campers who are vulnerable to cold in their body extremities can place an extra jacket, wool shirt, or blanket alongside their sleeping bag and use it during the colder hours, along toward morning.

Part Four

❦ ❦ ❦

BEYOND THE CONCRETE, NOISE, AND CROWDS

❦ ❦ ❦

✳ 10 ✳

Campsite Adventures

LAYOVER DAYS

In all wilderness-trip itineraries, layover days should be included. A day now and then, when the forward push halts and the crew takes time out to savor their paddling victory, adds not only a change of pace, but also a new element of attunement with the environment, of relaxation, an opportunity to pursue a hobby, a chance to know the satisfaction of achieving a planned goal.

Too often crew members plan a difficult and lengthy trip requiring the selection of a new site and the pitching of camp late each afternoon, and the trip turns into a competition with time and the environment—resulting in a frenzied push, the pace a race tempo of the life you had planned to leave behind.

It's an advantage to have necessary layover

days—to repair the canoe, to bake bread, to mend tent and gear, to sew, launder, or perhaps plain recuperate from a series of portages. The layover affords the opportunity for individual crew members to renew the feeling of "self," to relax from the close cooperation needed when cruising. It allows each one to get the feel of the new world, to absorb its riches through all the senses, to hear the new-found music of wind through pine needles, the lapping of waves on a rocky shore, the taste of new and different foods and beverages, to note the water, the land, and the cloud formations, and to react to the feeling of the sun on your face.

On solo walks, speech is unnecessary among the conifer cathedrals, where it seems that only you and a greater force abide. Then, something happens to time as we know it in daily life, for there comes a feeling to the wayfarer that the clock has stopped. You realize that you could be sitting on that large boulder in any century: in fact, you'll be startled at the feeling of completely belonging to the new environment, for the memory of work, of problems, and even of family fades away, and one understands the meaning of "going bush."

Perhaps take out the canoe alone, sit on the bottom with your back against the thwart while drifting along with a slow current or slight breeze, or just float motionlessly. Gaze around, read, or play the harmonica, the flute, or Jew's harp, and soon you'll identify with the world about you, become a part of it in a new-found experience. Your sensitivity will be sharpened. You'll see and feel more, live a degree more fully, at peace with yourself and the universe, and you'll experience a sensation of fulfillment and of pride at being a part of God's garden.

No one can anticipate what the experience will bring, for each tripper reacts in his distinctly personal way of identification with lesser creatures, to greater forces, and to inspiration.

In summer, the northland, like the tropics, becomes the embodiment of lushness in plant growth, the emergence of insects, the reproduction of animals, the mating of birds, the fecundity of water creatures. In the urgency to propagate the species, there seems to be a deadline against time, almost a frenzy in this throb of life that is evident everywhere. The warm season is condensed into a short period, and all of the native creatures seem to sense the impatient urge. I'm sure that the courtship of birds and of animals is shorter in the north. This spectacle, mostly of sound, once experienced is never forgotten.

Insect Pests

It is in this prolific season that various winged pests swarm into dominance, but fortunately, the cycles of some are short-lived. Mosquitoes, black flies and horseflies, no-see-ums, deer flies, midges, etc., need not detract from a wilderness experience, even though it is established that some campers more than others are bothered by them.

Effective control first begins with an adequately ventilated campsite. Areas to be avoided include: inland from the shore, dense vegetation, swampy places, low-lying and wet land where the mosquito was born.

Many effective repellents that have the endorsement of the U.S. Department of Agriculture are available: DDT in combination with malathion, and N-diethyl toluamide, available in pressurized cans. Apply the spray to the face, neck, hands, ankles, hat, clothing, boots, and to the inside of the tent as well as the netting.

Sprays offer almost complete protection with little irritation to the skin or injury to plastic frames of glasses. On portage trails or while doing camp chores, and on hot days when perspiration washes away the repellent, it must be reapplied often.

Bug bombs are used to spray the tent before bedtime. After all campers are in bed, should another treatment be necessary, spray lightly, and bury the nose and mouth in the crook of your arm or under the blanket to avoid inhalation of the spray.

"No-see-ums" and other tiny insects, able to get through regular mosquito netting, can be screened out with bobbinet, which has a finer mesh; finer yet is cheesecloth, although there's little air circulation through it.

Should you be without repellent, use a solution of nicotine water. Soak the tobacco of cigars, cigarettes, or pipe mixture in warm water, and apply the solution to the skin. Its staying power does not approximate that of commercial brands and it has to be applied more often. Plastering mud on the exposed parts of the body, as do animals, is another emergency protection.

Fishing

Fishing offers food, fun, and layover activity, but one should take every care to assure a satisfying experience. Remember, an empty canoe is less stable because of its higher center of buoyancy, and hooking a big fish, with its attendant excitement, will further endanger stability. The canoe should be emptied of all gear except fishing tackle. The stern paddler controls the canoe while his partner fishes. Kneeling is the recommended position for both.

In trolling situations, the fisherman sits on the bottom of the canoe, facing the paddler, and braces himself against the bow thwart (cushioned if desired). The rod tip is angled sternward, and the bait or lure is fished at different depths.

For shore line fishing, by casting into coves and pockets, at stumps or boulders, the fisherman takes a regular bow position in a kneeling position. In calm waters, he can sit on the seat, but never on the thwart.

Should you wish fish for dinner, walleyes head the gourmet list. I have discovered that a slow retrieve will decoy them, while the northern pike will disregard the lure—hence, slow retrieve for walleye, fast for northern pike and bass.

Fishing experts are legion, but statistically a few fishermen catch the majority of fish. Far from claiming to be an expert, some fishing procedures that have paid off in wilderness waters are listed.

Lake trout are a most sensitive-to-water-temperature fish, preferring cold water (approximately 40 degrees), and seek that layer in all times of the year. In spring, when the ice goes out, they can be found near the surface, and are caught on surface lures. As the warm weather heats the water, they gravitate to the deeper, colder waters. Progressively,

the lake trout can be found at ten, twenty, thirty feet. The Cree Indians in northern Ontario, who net fish in the summer, drop their nets in increasing depth to follow the lake trout's movements. Observation of their fishing depth can help the wilderness canoeist to locate fish—which can be quite difficult in the heat of summer. As it is difficult to troll for lake trout when they are in fifty to sixty feet of water, jigging is the best method to use. Special lures that attach to the top are dropped to the bottom, and jerked upward with the rod to send them shimming in circles. Seek out the deepest part of the lake—gen-

Veteran anglers know that trout often lurk in those pools below falls. The sternman paddles while the bowman fishes in one of Michigan's white water streams.
MICHIGAN TOURIST COUNCIL PHOTO

erally near a ledge, cliff, or high-banked shores.

The northern pike (called jackfish in Canada) can be located quite easily in weedy bays, among rushes, at the base of falls and rapids, and around reefs in open water. Trolling from one island to another is many times effective. This prolific fish has a wide temperature range preference from 55 to 75 degrees, and probably represents the biggest fish you'll catch in wilderness waters.

The walleye, being a member of the perch family, travels in schools, and once located, a mess can be caught. In the heat of summer, they stay deep (twenty to fifty feet), and any change in the natural bottom of a lake or river, as ledges, fractured layers of rock, submerged logs or boulders, are good places to probe. The walleyes are known to stateside fishermen as an evening and underwater feeder, but I have found them in all parts of wilderness lakes: along the shores, weed beds in the middle of lakes, in turbulent water—and they seem to bite in all parts of the day.

The walleye is mostly a minnow feeder, but will take worms with a spinner on a slow retrieve and numerous types of artificial lures. They give little fight in the preferred 62-degree temperature, but are delicious to eat. The fishermen can't have everything.

The advantage of wilderness fishing, with an added thrill, is that both the northern and walleye will take surface lures and smack them like bass.

The smallmouth bass, with the exception of stream trout, is probably the best scrapper of all wilderness fish. When hooked, the smallmouth will dive and dart, expending all its strength before capture. They prefer water of 65-degree temperature, with rocky, gravelly bottoms, and fast-moving water, too. Their preferred diet seems to be minnows, crayfish, and frogs. Bass bugs fished with a fly rod are effective.

The maskinonge, large-mouth (black) bass, and pan fish, with the exception of perch, not being native, are rarely found in wilderness waters.

There's no need to take a complete collection of lures, as a few basic ones will cover

Nogie's Creek is one of the best in the Kawartha Lakes, central Ontario, where smallmouth or large-mouth bass, pickerel, and pan fish abound, as well as maskinonge in the deeper waters.
CANADIAN GOVERNMENT TRAVEL BUREAU PHOTO

all fishing conditions. They include: spinners such as the June Bug, Abu Reflex, and Mepps; the Bass Oreno, an old and respected lure that dives and floats with the reel-in-and-pause retrieve; the Go Deeper River Runt, with its wobbly action that probes the bottom and brings in the fish; the Pikie Minnow with its slow, wobbling action, has been effective for fifty years; the Johnson Silver Minnow, with its slow, wobbly action, is ideal for slow and deep fishing, or for skittering over lily pads and through weeds.

The weedless spoon, with a pork chunk attached with red yarn, keeps from hanging up on rocks and weeds. The slow retrieve makes it a killer—to such degree, that I have seen northern pike leap out of the water when the bait was withdrawn. The red and white Daredevle, which outfished most spoons, is another lure for northern pike. It can be used in a fast skittering surface retrieve, a reel-in-and-pause retrieve, or in a jigging action near the bottom.

In the wilderness, live bait can include: grubs, caterpillars, grasshoppers, worms, leeches, crayfish, frogs, and minnows.

Emergency Lures

In wild-water fishing, many artificial lures can be contrived: wind flannel, wool, sack strands, or a shoelace around a bare hook for the body—add deer or squirrel fur for a tail or wings; add the tip of a feather for the hackle, tied near the eye of the hook—for artificial baits that will decoy unsophisticated fish. A pair of pliers grasped by a crew member holding the bare hook is a suitable vise for the fly-tying operation.

Other emergency lures include: spinners fashioned from the bowl end of a spoon, drilled so that a snap swivel in front and a treble hook at the rear can be attached. Pulled

through the water, the spoon lure will dart and flash in an appealing action.

It's possible, too, to fashion beer-can openers, bottle caps (pounded flat), clothespins, and even shaving brushes into deadly lures.

There's the old story that tells of a sly guide who won many bets by claiming that he could catch a pike on a lure without hooks. Needless to say, he received many takers—who lost. His method consisted of tying a long piece of red flannel (sometimes the part of a bright necktie) onto a line and casting it out into a likely pike haunt. The pike would strike the lure, and, because of the nature of its teeth (slanting backward), be unable to disgorge the soft cloth, and would be pulled in—without hooks.

Your contrived lures can be trolled by hand lines, without the use of conventional rod and reel. Another method of catching the fish is with the set or throw line, which is baited and cast from shore for overnight fishing. Bank fishing can also be practiced, in which the line is baited, cast out, and tied to a springy branch, which acts as a rod.

Emergency Snagging

In dire circumstances, the snagging of fish can be resorted to, simply by attaching to a line a treble hook and a sinker. Cast the line into the deep pool of a stream, or in a likely section of a lake, and jerk up when fish swim above it. The most productive time for snagging fish is when they congregate during spawning runs while they are on their beds or when migrating through narrow streams. Snagging is illegal, and is a method of angling used only for emergency survival purposes.

Some Precautions When Fishing

1. When casting from a canoe, or from the shore, use care not to endanger the nearby

Canoeing on the peaceful Chain o' Lakes.
DEPARTMENT OF NATURAL
RESOURCES, INDIANA, PHOTO

crew members. Check your backcast to make certain of adequate room.

2. Fly fishing requires a large clear area fore and aft, as the line feeds out on the backcast almost as far as in the forward cast.

3. Watch your footing, and figure out your strategy of landing a large fish, if hooked.

4. When wading—moss and rocks are very slippery—rather than standing on rocks, place each foot alongside of rocks, and brace them for solid footing. (Note: This method also is used when pulling the canoe through rock and shallow rivers.)

5. Keep your fishing tackle box closed and placed at your feet.

6. Tackle should include long-nosed pliers to remove hooks from pike, muskies, and lake trout. Also, cutter pliers to cut hooks when they become imbedded in clothing or in the scalp.

7. Fishhooks from lures and artificial flies, entering the human body, cause painful injuries. When a hook is too deeply imbedded in the flesh, it is advisable to force the hook through, instead of trying to pull it back against the barb. Snip off the shank of the hook, and with long-nosed pliers pull out the point and the barb. Wash the wound thoroughly with an antiseptic and then bandage it.

8. Proper overhand casting is safer than the side-swiping technique, and once a fish is hooked, the other fishermen reel in to keep from fouling lines.

9. When the fishing is exciting, canoeists often forget to watch the sky. Keep alert to changing weather conditions.

10. Don't embark on a fishing trip so long that getting back will be difficult. Plan to return to camp in time to clean fish, to collect

and stow tackle, and to prepare for cooking, etc.

What to Wear When Fishing

Expect to fall into the water, and dress accordingly:

1. Don't wear heavy shoes or restrictive clothes.

2. Wear loose-fitting clothing that permits freedom of movement and a broad-brimmed hat to protect the eyes from the sun and from fishhooks.

Fish Conservation

Becoming acquainted with conservation programs is an unexpected adventure (although it could be planned).

On one trip, we learned about the lamprey eel eradication program (sponsored jointly by the United States and Canada) on the Michipicoten River, near Wawa, Ontario, Canada, reached by the Algoma Central Railroad, which transported our canoe and gear. The fish biologist involved in the eradication program guided us to the Lake Superior feeder rivers and streams—the spawning grounds of the lamprey—to the electrically charged wires that kill them and rough fish, but not game fish.

On the second day, working from two large skiffs, we were invited to try our hand at another method of eradication. We motored to a small stream and went to work. The two boats, about twenty feet apart, were each equipped with a paddle-like metal plate attached to a long handle, and connected with an insulated wire to a series of batteries resting on the floor of the boat.

On signal, we were instructed to dip our metal plates into the stream bottom (we remained twenty feet apart). The electrical current was turned on from a control box in one of the boats. The baby lampreys, who spend their first years in the mud of quiet streams, were shocked out of their incubating habitat and killed, rising to the surface of the water. The lifeless forms were about three inches long, not much different from a skinny earthworm except for the bulbous head, which in adulthood would be used to suck out the juices, causing the death of game fish.

So effective was the lamprey eradication program, that today the lake trout, its main victim, has returned to the Great Lakes in former numbers, and commercial fishing for them has been resumed.

❧ 11 ❧

Meet the Natives:
Go Panning for Gold

Meet the People

THE enjoyment of the wilderness increases when you become acquainted with the trees, flowers, birds, animals, and fish in their natural settings, but most important, your land includes people—not many—and, as with lesser creatures, interaction with them, learning their livelihood problems, their drives and their dreams, is enriching.

Consider the sociology of the native Indian and the Eskimo. So remote are their habitations, that in this twentieth century they have never seen a traffic light, a carton of milk, or a two-story structure. Meet the occasional white man who has turned his back on a former way of life to "live deep and suck out all the marrow of life, to live so sturdily and Spartan-like as to put to rout all that was not life, to cut a broad swath and shave close, to

drive life into a corner, and reduce it to its lowest terms. . . ." (Thoreau)

One wilderness trip took us into the northern Ontario hinterland, where we met a resourceful and determined white native whose bush skills—shooting, fishing, paddling, and drinking, along with great physical strength—excelled those of the local Indians, and he had become a legend in his own time. He had set out to compete with the local Hudson's Bay Post by setting up his own trading post and purchasing furs from the Indians, bringing them great distances with his payment of a few cents more for each fur. His fortunes rose and fell with the years, and although our acquaintance never realized the dream of putting the Hudson's Bay Post out of business, he was, nevertheless, a spirit-stirring personality who, with gusto, furnished the fillip to withstand an austere world better.

The exact opposite was a French padre who

97

Scouting the new-found neighborhood.
PROVINCE OF QUEBEC FILM BUREAU PHOTO

was meeting the needs of the adults and children as he served the Indians. Several days out of Deer Lake Post, we reached Sandy Lake and saw the White Hudson's Bay Post buildings perched on a rise beyond the sloping stone ramps at the shores, gleaming in the sun. After the introductory amenities and

pitching camp, the post manager mentioned Father Dassault.

"Take the trail behind the fur storage shed and bear left if you wish to visit him."

Up and down the rocky path, through dense growth, we walked until the woods opened into the father's realm, and we stood transfixed by the sight of several acres of cleared land, its rich soil, deep and furrowed, covered with the healthy leafage of beans, cabbages, potatoes, and corn—produce befitting the center of Iowa. This rugged wilderness area lying above the fifty-second parallel in Canada can be an inhospitable land, characterized by turbulent water, chaotic rock, and a profusion of scrub trees and muskeg, fighting for the meager nutriment of soil—a land not known for growing vegetables.

Tall and thin, with twinkling eyes, the padre was one of the most serene men I have ever met: no worry lines creased his face, no urgency charged his voice, and from his movements and his speech, it was obvious that neither time, pressures, his lot in life, nor the sins of man haunted him. His voice was soft and comforting to us and to the Indian boys playing in the yard. As we sat in the kitchen, the padre told of clearing the trees, of scraping the precious soil from the forest floor, of fertilizing the garden with jackfish (pike), and of eventually being able to grow the vegetables so greatly needed by the Indian children.

We were the first white men to visit the Little Grand Rapids Hudson's Bay Post and Indian Village in Manitoba in fifteen years.

At twilight, a booming sound from the council ring ended our getting-acquainted talk with the post personnel and the fire warden. We arrived in time to witness the tuning-up procedure of a huge drum, about three feet in diameter, turned toward the fire to tighten and to shrink the skin to proper tone. As the chief drummer pounded the skin

Wild rice beds give an interest to the water scene.
OUTBOARD BOUND PHOTO

in single, testing blows, the Indian families beached their canoes and streamed toward the council hill.

Soon, four drummers took their positions around the drum, which had been lashed to four upright poles to honor the white Voyageurs who had unexpectedly dropped in from the South.

We stood on the perimeter of the group with Fred Moar, an Englishman with an Indian wife, as he interpreted the unfolding ceremony. Chief John Keeper and his squaw were the first to dance around the council ring—the signal for all to join. In simple one-two beat, the drummers pounded the skin, and the Indians responded, stomping around and around the drum.

After many dances in the growing darkness, Chief Keeper rose and spoke eloquently of the tribe's history and traditions in obvious effort to inspire the teen-agers who were, we surmised, straying from old ways (the generation gap occurring in wilderness areas, too!).

The giant heartbeat of the drum intensified, and the dancers responded to its primitive message. Chief Keeper rose again to thank the visitors for the gift of tea which was being ladled out of a huge pot, for adults and children alike, and for the twist tobacco that bucks and squaws scooped out of a huge leather pouch, tamped in their pipes, and sucked with gusto.

After midnight, a full moon rose above the serrated pine treetops, and the feral beat and the thump of moccasined feet melted our self-consciousness; we selected squaws, old and young, to dance to the primitive spell. Many dances later, the simple rhythm was no longer novel, alien, or incongruous. We danced every dance, shouted the explosive "Hu, Hu!" to the thunder that resounded louder and louder, faster and faster, for we had entered the Indians' kingdom of vibrational energy, and the light in our faces showed that we were happy to pass that threshold.

When the chief and his wife danced once

Indian girl meeting a white man for the first time in her life.

JOHN W. MALO PHOTO

again to signify the end of the Drum Dance, for all of us it was a reluctant, "Three o'clock in the morning," for we had played on the edge of a feral culture for a brief moment, and I can understand the phenomena of a white man "going bush."

Other fleeting friendships along the wilderness trail return in memory to hearten frustrating hours:

Enjoying tea and cookies with a teacher and his wife (from Montreal), who held school for two months (July and August) when the children were congregated at the posts, and their talk of adult Indians who quietly stalked into the classroom, stood near the door for hours without comment, then as silently stole away.

A lumber mill superintendent, far up the Algoma Central country, proudly showing us his complete operation: bunkhouses, kitchen, dining hall, ball field, the lumberjacks of many nationalities, sizes, and temperaments, the topping, felling, trimming, and stacking of tall trees; then, because it was "a bad year for bears," promptly going out to the garbage dump and immediately shooting a bear to prove his point.

Prospectors in the hinterlands who, regardless of their years of frustration, the meager rewards, the sufferance, still travel the back roads, forever confident that their long bonanza trail will meet with the end of the rainbow.

Gold Panning

In this age of automation, it is still possible to emulate the prospectors of 1849 by panning in many of the gold-bearing streams of the United States and Canada, and within an eight-hour day, in suitable sand, to pan several dollars' worth of gold.

Every outdoorsman (their families, too) should have the experience of working a pan, reducing its sand to a gold flake, scooping up more sand, more flakes, and gradually seeing a small treasure accumulate.

Creek gold is the most easily discovered by panning methods which require little outlay of money and no cumbersome equipment. All you need are the ideal gold pan, 14½ inches in diameter at the top, with sloping sides that give a bottom diameter of 8½ inches, and a depth of three inches. Ambitious prospectors feel that a smaller pan permits easier and faster operation, which in the long run enables them to work more sand without tiring.

A commercial pan costs about $1.50, but a frying pan without a handle, or a shallow metal washpan will do. Whichever you use, make sure that the bottom has been scoured clean. Heat-treat your pan before use by placing it in an oven for an hour, at about 400 degrees. A shovel is needed for scooping the sand; a No. 2 round-point is recommended. A magnifying glass, a powerful magnet, and some plastic containers and canvas bags represent the tools of the trade.

Your equipment in order, with some horse sense, a strong back, and ambition prodding you, you're ready for the gold streams!

The distribution of gold is extremely irregular, and heartening news for the amateur is the fact that rich gold (and uranium) finds were made by those who knew too little ecology and stream savvy to be deterred from trying. The rarity of gold makes it valuable, and finding it is a heart-warming accomplishment.

Let nature help you. Ordinary erosion breaks up the rock, releasing the ores of gold. First, the gold-bearing rock in hills and moun-

tains, loosened by weathering—rain, freezing, and chemical action—is washed down and the swirling water sorts out the material with which gold is mixed. Thus, we find the stream movement promoting a natural sorting of the gold and heavy material. The gold does not travel far in the stream when the velocity diminishes. It settles to the bottom in fissures, sink holes, in natural riffles, or in the long sand bars.

In such areas, the material is given a first-class panning—circulation and grinding—by the current, and becomes entrapped in the holes or thrown out by the whirling action of water, and deposited in quieter waters below.

Often the heavy portions of sand bars indicate the presence of heavy ores, including gold. Dry sand bars also merit investigation; the ones where a drought or change of main channel have left them high and dry.

The Fortymile River in Alaska winds through land rich in gold mining history.
PHOTO COURTESY U.S. DEPARTMENT OF THE INTERIOR: BUREAU OF LAND MANAGEMENT

The upper portions of streams are rich in gold possibilities; the lower reaches are not, for as the gold moves downstream, it is more diffused, less concentrated, finely divided, and not so rich. As clay will sometimes trap gold specks, so too will moss; and prospectors in the West collect the moss that grows along streams, burn it, and pan the residue which sometimes yields pay dirt.

Even for children, it is not difficult to operate a pan of sand and reduce it to concentrate:

1. Scoop a shovelful of likely looking sand from the long, dark sand bars of a stream and place it in your pan.

2. Dip the pan into the water to cover its contents, and permit the light material to float out.

3. Stir the mixture with your fingers to break up the lumps and to wet all particles.

4. Pour off the muddy water.

5. Dip your pan again for clear water.

6. Throw out all large stones and pebbles.

7. With both hands holding the pan (on opposite sides) under water, vigorously shake the pan in a circular motion, and the lighter mud, mica, and silt will float off, while the heavy particles will settle.

8. After another round of circular panning (under water), raise up the pan, tilt it to 30 to 40 degrees, so that more light material (in suspension) washes over the lip of the pan.

9. With one hand, vigorously pat your diminishing sand sample to aid in further settling the heavy particles.

10. Again dip the pan, and continue to swirl, but this time the pan is in a tilted position, so that the swirling water splashes out more top-riding sand.

After several sequences of dipping the pan below water, sloshing it over the edge of the pan, the remaining material will begin to appear much darker than the original sample. Proceed with more gentle action, as you are zeroing in on the valuable conglomerate —pour off, dip the pan, resume swirling. After six to ten such operations, your shovelful of sand has been reduced to a few ounces of concentrated material at the bottom edge, consisting of heavy sand and minerals—including gold if you're lucky!

Gold particles, dust or flake, that are recognizable, can be removed from the pan by touching them with a dry finger and placing them in a small plastic vial filled with water. Touching the water in the vial with your finger will release the gold speck from it, and the gold falls to the bottom to launch your gold-collecting adventure.

In essence, the panning procedure is an attempt to glean the heavy gold by eliminating all the lighter materials in the conglomerate. Toward this end, practice at home by throwing about twenty or more small ball bearings or shotgun BBs from a No. 2 shell into your pan, and mix with sand. The swirling, pouring off water and sand, adding water —in repeated sequence—should leave only the heavy balls and a little sand. Aim to retain ninety to one hundred percent of the simulated gold to qualify as a panner for the creeks and streams.

Further separation of unnoticeable gold is made by drying your concentrate over a campfire, or by spreading it over a board or smooth rock. While the sample is drying, begin work on a new batch of sand. Treat the samples, when dry, with the magnet. Magnetic black sands adhere to the magnet, but to prevent the fuzzy particles of metal from sticking, cover the ends of the magnet with cellophane or light cloth. In this way, when the magnet is withdrawn, the unwanted particles will drop off. The lighter sands of a non-metallic nature can be cleared from your gold dust by blowing lightly across it.

Panned gold varies in color from a light yellow to a dull, coppery, lusterless hue, some-

Return to camp after a day of exploring Quetico Park, Ontario.
ONTARIO DEPT. OF TOURISM & INFORMATION PHOTO

times nearly black, as coloration is affected by its environment of different minerals.

For permanent proof of your discovery, take your "poke" to an assayer, who will melt down the grains into a single nugget, called a "button," which can be mounted on a tie clasp, ring, or stickpin. Should your digging and panning result in a net weight of an ounce or more of gold (lucky you), the United States mint will buy the gold at the standard price of thirty-five dollars per ounce (or whatever is the current rate).

The serious prospector plans his strategy long before reaching the waters of gold, and as many of the desired streams are located in remote wildernesses, your camping knowhow, equipment, gear, grub lists, and survival knowledge must be adequate.

In researching your trip, write in advance for information:

For Canadian information, the Chief Gold Commissioner, Victoria, B.C., or the Department of Mines and Technical Surveys, Ottawa, Ontario. Each of the provinces also has its own Department of Mines at its capital city.

In the United States, the county seat of your operation is always a good source of information: the assessor will give you information about claims and past yields. The Bureau of Mines at any of the state capitals will answer any preliminary questions, and it is proper to ask for information and reports on the present gold situation as well as on known gold locations.

The United States Department of the Interior, Bureau of Mines, Washington, D.C., is another source.

Map research in libraries will yield good roads and streams, and will serve to indicate accessibility. Sources include: state and federal agencies, the state park boards, the U.S. Forest Service regional offices, and the National Park administration.

12

Wild
Waters

THE wilderness traveler faces many challenges as he safely paddles the canoe with its passengers, gear, and equipment along turbulent rivers, on shallow streams, on large lakes, in high winds, and portages around turbulent rapids and waterfalls.

There's something special about a river: it has a different meaning to each challenger, for its character changes from day to day, from season to season, from year to year (just as each lake has its distinct individuality). One does not establish rules applying to all conditions, but delineates methods for meeting various ones.

Take No Watercourse for Granted

Many of the reactions of a canoeist to atypical conditions become subconscious and automatic, and the more mileage behind him, the more adaptable he becomes: however, a wise

canoeist never takes a familiar watercourse for granted as one does an old friend—and that can be considered a basic rule for all wilderness canoeing.

Always Use Hindsight

When traveling on new waters, hindsight—regularly looking back, actually scouting the water you've just paddled through—will be a tremendous advantage in orientation when coming back over the same trail (whether or not by plan or by some emergency need) with the least expenditure of time and effort.

Note especially any streams entering the river. If you haven't checked the shore lines by hindsight on route, on the return trip, the fork of two streams may be confusing. Many northland rivers have dead-end arms, and it is disheartening to paddle up for a mile or two, only to find the stream ending abruptly.

Choosing the outside edge of the stream where the water is less turbulent.
SASKATCHEWAN BUREAU OF NATURAL RESOURCES PHOTO

The Berens River in Ontario, Canada, has many such dead-end arms, and we soon learned how to distinguish them. On the shores of the main stream, debris has piled up from the current at ice-break-up time. The force pushes outward and upward the logs, leaves, and the branches that become lodged against boulders and tree trunks on the up-stream side.

Another method of determining the main river channel is to check the underwater weeds: if they stand up straight, that usually denotes a dead-end arm; they bend and waver in the main-stream current.

PADDLE BEFORE DAWN

Another basic rule to follow: regardless of weather in the land of swift rivers and large lakes, whenever the schedule requires it, the canoeist arises at dawn and paddles during the early hours. In inclement weather, because violent storms seldom occur before nine o'clock in the morning, he arises before dawn to paddle in the early hours.

WHITE WATER

Like precious gems, rapids are rated on a scale, from one (easy) to six (of utmost difficulty, near limit of navigability).

Shooting white water in a canoe or kayak is one of the most harrowing sports known, and in the wilderness there's no Army Corps of Engineers' river gauge to notify you of the water's height and velocity.

The specialized craft used on roaring rivers, past sharp rocks and granite walls, requires a polyester resin reinforced with fiber glass.

The pilot needs a scuba suit and a crash helmet; the craft is empty of duffel and gear.

This sport usually is practiced only in specific areas where help is readily available, which is not the case in wilderness travel, for there controlled white water with rescue crews nearby is not available.

Only the expert canoeist should attempt to shoot rapids. For most situations, it is far wiser to take out as soon as the rumble of rapids is heard or a rising white spray is seen. Sometimes the decision to portage or to shoot a rapid must be made quickly, especially on a river that narrows and races, and the drop of the water over obstructing rocks comes quickly.

Sometimes you can come upon rapids without advance visual or audio evidence. Once, in northern Ontario, while cruising down an unnamed river, broad and placid, on the right I noticed a break in the orderly shore line. Cruising farther, on the left bank, too, the shore line was broken. "Falls!" I quickly yelled. As we made shore, we noticed the ten-foot falls. The river bottom of solid rock fractured clean—as if sheared by a giant saw. The water fell smoothly over the sharp corner with no visual evidence of turbulence. A few ledges on the vertical wall supported vegetation, like flower pots surrounded by cascading water. We aptly named the phenomenon *Flower Pot Falls*.

In running a fast river, the wilderness canoeist must, by knowing the significance of each visual condition—the volume, speed, rips, haystacks, and foam—ascertain whether or not the unloaded canoe can be brought safely through, and translate that knowledge into action.

Empty canoe being taken through rough water, while gear is transported overland.
MICHIGAN TOURIST COUNCIL PHOTO

Judgments must be made only after a close look at the ways of the moving waters. The entire course of travel through turbulent water must be planned—to the very thinking through of the paddle strokes that will be necessary.

Scouting rapids from the shore gives insight into a run that cannot be secured from a canoe.

Where the slightest doubt occurs, think about lining or about portaging.

The canoeist in the wilderness must be aware of and respect the tons of force generated by fast-moving water:

1. From past experience, he knows that the force is fastest in the middle of a river and at the top.

2. That it is slowest at the sides of the river and on the bottom.

3. The flow pattern is affected by cliff banks, by ledges, fallen trees, and rocks.

4. Obstructions deflect the current and generate variations in water velocity.

5. The powerful surge of water under fallen trees is especially dangerous.

6. Coming broadside into a stationary object with water surging underneath it results in a very quick capsize.

7. Fast-moving water is slowed down by a boulder, piles up, and is deflected, creating an eddy behind the boulder. This peaceful stretch in a turbulent current can work for the canoeist, serve as a welcome resting place. Strong paddling will get the canoe safely through the sharp eddy line to quiet water that gently flows counter to the main current.

In general, follow the main channel, which has the fastest current, usually is deep and unobstructed, always making sure that there is a safe way out from it. When several passages loom, stay with the main current, following the smooth tongues of fast water. Look

Little need to worry, once the favorable route through rapids is determined.
MINNEAPOLIS *Tribune* PHOTO

Shooting the Cedar Rapids on the Flambeau River.
WISCONSIN NATURAL RESOURCES DEPT. PHOTO

and plan ahead, noting the fast approaching challenges, and prepare to revise the course as situations develop. There are no set rules, but rather general cautions that must be adapted to conditions, of which no two sets are alike.

In reading water, note that a "Λ" pointed upstream has a rock at its point; and a "V" pointed downstream marks the watercourse between two upstream rocks and its slick water, if wide enough, can be run.

Obviously, the best way to run a river is to stay with the deep water in its center on straight stretches, on the outside on curves, and on "S" curves which demand study because of their characteristic of piling up sand bars on either side and in the center of the "S" curves. All rivers, of course, are not so predictable: rocks, logs, and ledges do tricks

to the water, requiring fast steerage and control to bring the canoe through.

In a strong current, the canoe is unstable in the sense that its streamlined design will tend to increase any turn it has begun. In turning or in sideslipping, the stern slews around faster than the bow. The turn is best checked by the sternman: bringing the stern behind the bow is his everlasting chore in fast water. In many instances, although he doesn't determine course, he steers, sometimes frantically, to follow the bow around obstructions.

To avoid trouble in rock- or log-strewn water, the bowman has the responsibility of quickly making his decision in order to see the entire canoe through—not just his end! Once past the obstruction, the bowman must be concerned about the middle and the stern of the canoe. Will there be enough time for the sternman to bring the canoe around? When approaching obstructions, the bowman cannot wait too long to pull or push his end over. The principle of alignment of canoe with the current is the eternal concern of the bowman.

The vigilant bowman must make the decision, yelling "Right" or "Left" of a looming obstruction, then quickly reacting with a pry or draw stroke.

The sternman counters with the opposite stroke to bring his end in line. The canoe slides past the obstruction and there is no need for extra speed.

In narrow, tortuous channels, the bowman calls upon many strokes, quickly and decisively drawing, prying, sweeping, braking, to avoid obstructions and to keep the canoe properly pointed. Water force does tricks to a canoe. Sometimes there is a subtle sideways slide that soon takes the canoe broadside downstream. If every paddle stroke for cor-

rection fails, and the canoe comes to a thudding halt against a log or boulder, the bottom tends to roll in water-wheel fashion and water pours in over the gunwale (if the hang-up is serious), the bowman quickly jumps into the water upstream of the canoe, holds onto the gunwale, and tries to lift the canoe off the obstruction. Then, holding the line (painter), before boarding if possible, he attempts to line the canoe with the current.

Sometimes, when coming broadside against an obstruction, the canoeists move to the downstream side of the canoe to bring up the gunwale facing the water's surge. In this way, the water will slide under the canoe and not swamp it.

If possible, one canoeist jumps upon the obstruction. With painter in hand, he pulls the canoe alongside, in the current, and eases it around into the calm eddy below the obstruction.

Shooting the slick waters in the Sioux Lookout Area, Ontario.
ONTARIO DEPT. OF TOURISM

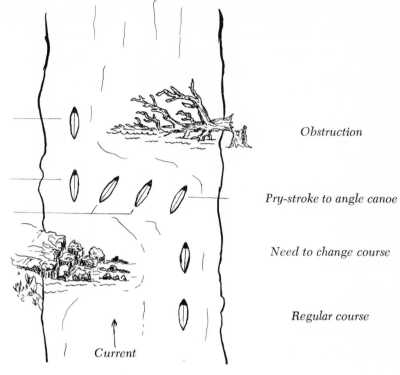

Continue new course

Canoe aligned with current

Back-paddling against current

Obstruction

Obstruction

Pry-stroke to angle canoe

Need to change course

Regular course

Current

BACK-PADDLING FERRY

FERRYING OR SETTING

Ferrying (setting) is a technique used when it becomes necessary to cross over a strong current to the opposite side of a river. Very often on the route side of a river, the opening closes up with obstructions and it is necessary quickly to change your course to avoid letting the current carry you into the obstruction.

The basic technique calls for back-paddling to the opposite shore at an angle to the current. The paddling angle will depend on the speed of the river and on the strength of the paddlers, but a 30-degree angle is a good average in this battle of backward motion and the downstream flow of the current.

The ferry is initiated by the sternman, who,

with a quick pryaway or back sweep angles his end of the canoe toward the opposite shore.

The pry-away stroke is a fast-water stroke, a version of the push-away, but power considerations require more forceful action to bring the bow or stern around. Slide the paddle vertically, deep into the water, or angle it under the canoe, and pry off the widest part of the canoe. With both hands, pull the paddle shaft to a little beyond vertical. Go back for another pry. Recover by feathering the blade under water—because that is faster than the aerial recovery.

Both paddlers immediately back-paddle to hold the angle against the current, using sweep or draw strokes on opposite sides of the canoe. Once the bowman sees that the obstruction has been cleared, he draws the canoe into alignment with the current for safe continuation on the new-found forward course.

Forward Ferry

The forward ferry is preferred by some canoeists. Spin the canoe about so that the bow points upstream. The speed is a factor here, as there is some time and distance lost in turning the canoe. The canoeists paddle forward in the natural way, and many find it more natural and powerful than the back ferry.

After the current has been crossed, spin the canoe about for continuation of the downstream travel.

For landing in a fast current, either the back or forward ferry can be used. The first canoeist ashore takes the painter with him to secure the canoe. The painters should be inboard under the bow and stern decks, coiled and tied with a piece of shock cord. When landing, there's no need to untie or to untangle the painter as the bowman jumps ashore.

Other White Water Conditions

The long, uniform drop, with plenty of water racing over submerged boulders, produces a series of large, standing waves called *haystacks*. In shooting haystacks, the canoeists change the head-on—lined with current—course to quarter the waves (as in open-lake travel) to permit the canoe to ride each wave and to ship less water.

In situations where river-running plans go awry and control is temporarily lost, it may be necessary to run a passage backward. This is especially true of wilderness travel because of added complications—large canoe, narrow, rock-strewn rivers, weight, etc.—which make the canoe more vulnerable to hang-ups which may spin it.

In such situations, keep cool, disregard the embarrassment, and recover as soon as possible to continue with the bow leading, aligned with the current.

In quick water, the only paddling position is kneeling, not the high kneeling position, but squatting down on your heels with hips or lower back braced against a thwart or the edge of the canoe seat. The position offers a strong base and a lower center of gravity that gives more power to strokes and safety in rock or log collisions.

On hang-ups, a downward thrust of the paddle or pole pushes up the canoe bottom, easing the weight and floating it over the obstruction. Using the paddle as a pole to push the canoe is rarely done; rather, reverse the paddle and hold the blade. Apply the grip end to the bottom of the stream or to the rock. Because of its awkwardness, this expedient soon will convince you that you should carry a sapling pole in preparation for such a maneuver.

A few commands are needed in teaming up to bring a canoe through: "Right," "Left," "Back," and "Brake," are simple enough, but their execution under pressure is another matter, requiring a lot of practice. Should a campsite offer a mild rapid, spend some time teaming up on strokes, on white-water skills, and techniques. Soon it becomes apparent that one must work harder in swift water when strokes seem to be ineffective.

SWIMMING SKILLS

In all duckings, remember that the body is buoyant and that a relaxed body, with slow movements, abets buoyancy. Almost every person can float by using the U.S. Navy (vertical float): simply extend the arms sideward, arch the back, place the head backward as far as possible so that just the face is above water, remain motionless, and bide your time.

Canoeing the Wolf River as it races hastily by near Langlade, Wisconsin.
WISCONSIN CONSERVATION DEPT. PHOTO

The legs will probably sink, but the chest and the face will remain above water. Slight movement of the hands (sculling) and feet (scissors kick) will help those who do not float as readily as most. Cases on record reveal that prior to rescue, swimmers have floated for many hours in this fashion.

The surface dive, enabling a swimmer to submerge six, eight, or ten feet to recover objects on the bottom, is a skill that has helped me innumerable times—to retrieve an overboard camera, a ditty bag, cooking utensils, and snagged fishing lures (in short supply) needed to capture a food supplement. The skill requires a jackknifing of the body, bringing up the feet toward the hands, hips up, then flipping up the legs skyward to send the body head first in a vertical dive. A lazy flip will place the body on an angled dive, making accuracy difficult.

Treading water, various swimming strokes and kicks, lifesaving carries, and endurance in water are additional skills that supply a wealth of confidence to the canoeist when traveling the hinterland areas.

If You Capsize in White Water

When capsized or swamped, try to hold onto your paddle, and immediately jump upstream of the canoe. The standard canoe fills up rapidly with a ton of water, and the occupants must never allow themselves to be caught between this force and a fixed obstruction.

If possible, ride the canoe, but abandon it quickly should your safety be endangered.

Don't try to swim in a strong current: turn over and use an elementary backstroke, with the feet leading, knees slightly flexed to absorb the shock of underwater boulders and to ward off others.

Gradually work out of the current and into shallow water. Your laced sneakers and clothing offer some protection.

After paddlers are safely ashore, that's the time to salvage the canoe. It has a way of coming to shore at the bottom of rapids.

Since you never transport your equipment, gear, and grub in a canoe through white water, the above is based on an empty canoe.

𝒳 13 𝒳

Wild
Woods

TAKE a solo hike on a layover day? Be careful. Do not stray too far from the campsite.

That warning is based on solid wilderness lore and a biological fact: the human body is not symmetrical; there is a difference in length between the two arms and between the two legs—in both cases the right being the longer. Also, the right shoulder is bigger than the left, and most people are right-handed. The difference in length between the limbs seems to affect the hiking, paddling, rowing, and swimming of most persons.

We Walk in Circles

In an open expanse, a hiker will walk in a wide arc—right or left—and should the distance be long, he will complete a full circle. Check your own footprints on a field of snow or on a broad expanse of sand, on which no obstacles or landmarks appear, and notice the curving pattern.

The reason for this is not explained adequately only by anatomical structure; there may be a spiraling influence centered in the brain of all living creatures.

This deviation from a straight path is increased when wearing a heavy packsack, by strong winds, the hot sun, by rain, snow, difficult terrain, or by a stepped-up pace. Deviation in walking around obstacles tends to follow a consistent pattern—either left or right, depending on the individual. On long journeys, the accumulation of deviation can reach substantial proportions: therefore, after an extensive meditation or an exploration hike, don't feel confident that you can make a beeline for camp and reach it by dead reckoning. You can't!

LOST IN THE WOODS!

Your solo hike is finished as the day ebbs. Whether it was a fishing trip to some isolated pothole, gold panning, or probing the hills with a Geiger counter—your activity completely engrossed you. It's time to return to camp, but you didn't bring a compass, you paid little attention to your route, to the distance, or your whereabouts. Walking toward camp, you suddenly realize that the sun seems to be setting in the east! The terrain is different, known landmarks have disappeared, and your world suddenly becomes ominously quiet. Then it hits you, personally. "I am lost!"

Never before have you spent a night alone in the wild; you've spent a lifetime within earshot of other persons. You're unnerved. Will you become panic-stricken, letting fear and desperation blot out a rational solution? Will all the outdoor knowledge you possess go by the boards?

A way back to camp, along known landmarks, may be nearby. All that is required of you to find it is to climb the nearest height of land or to climb a tree and take a look around. Nothing looks familiar?

"I'm lost!" Acknowledge the fact, but don't panic. Sit down and relax! Listen to the sounds, and think about them. Ask: "Do I hear my crew mates?" "Is that a whistle blast?" "Do I hear the sounds of rapids or of waterfalls?" "Voices borne on the wind? From what direction?" Keep cool. If you begin to sweat, you're losing the battle.

Alone and lost? There's only one immediate decision: prepare to spend the night in the wild. The fortitude, training, and experience that you have taken with you into the bush will determine your ability to face up to the situation and to meet it; but many campers, through overpowering fear of being lost, re-sort to unreasoning flights, to thrashing frantically through the brush, to driving themselves beyond the limits of their strength, tearing their clothes, stubbing their toes, or spraining an ankle. Being completely tuned out, their seeing and hearing faculties become worthless.

The dangers lie not in the environment—in animals, starvation or loss of sleep—but within you—fright, desperation, complete exhaustion, and shock, which the *American Red Cross First Aid Textbook* informs us, ". . . affects both mind and body. It is a depressed state of all bodily functions caused by failure of the circulation. The degree of shock may be anything from a mild form, lasting only a short time, to severe forms, which frequently result in death."

Severe shock results in faintness and weakness and sometimes dizziness and nausea. The face and the extremities become ashen, cold, and moist with perspiration. The eyes appear vacant, while they dilate. Vomiting often occurs. The shallow and rapid breathing becomes irregular. These conditions, without a serious injury, are largely self-imposed and obviously neither prepare the lost camper for a rational solution to his safety nor ensure his survival.

With a frank acknowledgment of the situation, the odds of surviving the night are great, and the morning, with a full day ahead in which to find your way back, will reassure you. In the meantime, your crew members will begin a full-scale search. Their task will be simpler if you stay put; don't become a moving target for your crew, who certainly will be looking for you.

There's too much romanticism written about building a Robinson Crusoe habitation, snaring wild animals for food, catching fish in some primitive way, becoming a "nature boy," and living in pristine glory through a "being lost" experience.

Face the facts: "I won't be lost for long." "I don't need an elaborate shelter, a fluffy bed." "As for food, the average person can live without food for thirty days, more or less, as long as water is available."

EMERGENCY SHELTERS

The simplest shelter may be made from a conifer with low branches. Check the ground under it for dryness, and crawl there for shelter. Or, pull together a bunch of branches— hemlock browse—or moss for cover.

Take advantage of a rocky ledge, a cave, or cliff as a rude shelter. A reflector fire in front, kept roaring, will lift the spirit in a feeling of warmth and security. Should you be carrying a poncho (and shouldn't you?), convert it into an adequate shelter. Set it up by stringing a slender pole or cord between two trees, three to four feet above the ground, and attach one edge of the poncho to it. Anchor the opposite edge to the ground with rocks. Some boughs, dry moss, grass, or leaves on the ground under the poncho will serve as a soft bed. Build a reflector fire in front of the shelter to deflect the heat toward you. Don't wrap yourself in the poncho, as its waterproof property will condense bodily moisture, soak your clothes, and keep the coldness inside.

A primitive shelter is easily and quickly constructed. When properly set up, it offers warmth, comfort, and protection from rain. This bear-den type of shelter involves the cutting (halfway through) of a sapling and the bending of the bushy end to the ground. Trim the underside branches to open up a snug retreat. Insulate the ground with moss or browse cover. A reflector fire will give sufficient warmth for some sleep.

An Indian shelter can be constructed with no tools except a sheath knife. Cut a slim, twelve-foot pole, sharpen one end, and jam it into the ground. Place the other end in the fork of a small tree about four feet from the ground, giving an angled ridge pole. Cut limbs of young hemlocks with tufts of foliage, and shingle them over the ridge pole to form an inverted V-shaped roof. Build up the thatch of fanlike boughs, laying them bottom side up toward the ridge pole, overlapping the thatch as you proceed. A bright reflector fire in front will direct the heat to the bedding below.

Your shelter set up, you slow down. Take it easy! You have time to kill before darkness falls. Next, take the wood-supply chore. Don't try to scrounge firewood. Burn big logs in two. The pine knots on decaying trees, such as hemlock branches, contain a concentration of resin, and they will burn for hours.

With the reassurance of the warm fire, drowsiness probably sets in. Soon you will fall asleep. During the night, as the fire burns low, chill sets in, and you'll almost certainly awaken from the need to urinate, which urgency, biologically, is based on the fact that the body must regularly give off fluids through perspiration or urination. When awake, stoke the fire. Then build up the body heat by jogging in place, flapping your arms, and doing some deep knee bends. The generated body heat may sustain you for another hour or so of sleep. The night may seem long, but you'll be able to welcome the dawn.

GETTING UNLOST

Don't set a mental timetable for your rescue, and you won't be disappointed if you must hole up in the same general area for another night. Occupy yourself by improving your bed and your shelter, keep the fire going with a lot of green leaves to serve as a smoke signal. In all forests, smoke is the danger sign,

TEMPORARY SHELTERS

the most watched-for eventuality, and it is the mission of fire wardens to spot it and to investigate its source as soon as possible.

Place your brightest clothes in the most conspicuous place: tree branch, shrub, cliff, etc.—anywhere it might attract attention. Should a bush or searching plane fly near, hail it by waving your shirt while standing in an open area. As the hours pass, take a nap in the warm sun. This is in line with the prescribed treatment for shock (the lost person is potentially a patient in shock, and should treat himself as such), whether or not the symptoms are present. The treatment, briefly, is to lie down with the head twelve to eighteen inches lower than the feet to facilitate blood flow to the vital organs—heart and brain.

Conserve body heat with protection underneath from cold and damp ground.

Thirst, due to the drying out of the soft tissues lining the mouth, can aggravate, and is relieved by merely sipping small amounts instead of gulping down large quantities of water. Sugary food, such as candy, further induces thirst. Munching a leaf stem, twigs, dried fruit, or sucking a fruit pit, are the preferred thirst quenchers.

You may wish to try to retrace your steps, and sometimes this is quite easy and successful. On a cold autumn hike, when generated heat prompted me to place my mittens in my mackinaw pocket, later I discovered that one had dropped out, and proceeded to look for it. Retracing my steps, I recalled much of my meandering path: skirting a fallen oak, passing a thick dogwood patch, walking through a small clearing, circling an ice-encrusted cattail pond to the bank of a stream, and downstream on the high bank. There it was. The mitten had dropped out as I photographed the semi-solid state of water: a thin sheet of ice above, the gurgling water below. I am aware, of course, that had I been in panic at being lost, many of these rational recollections would not have come so easily.

Reach down deep inside to come up with a tenacity to save yourself. The disbeliever has many problems: loss of confidence, fighting himself, the weather, the time of day, overexertion, and perhaps, mental fatigue. Experienced outdoorsmen become accustomed to emergency situations, recognize their errors, correct them, and hang on. During most of our wilderness trips, while navigating to inadequate maps, we were lost many times, not knowing exactly where we were on a map at a given moment, but by forging onward, that large lake, the river fork, or a feeder stream loomed ahead, and all was well—until another navigational problem developed.

Long before you go into the wilderness, it is good conditioning to ponder, "What if I should get lost?" Then ask yourself: "Am I afraid of being alone?" "Afraid of the darkness?" "Of strange noises?" Just thinking about all of the ramifications of the eventuality has positive value. The process will prepare you for the physical and mental strain of such an actual crisis—should it ever occur.

There are many cases on record of children being lost for hours, sometimes days, and because they were fascinated by their newfound world, became engrossed in nature observations, occupied themselves in simple activities, and didn't panic, they were found safe and happy. The prospect of being lost is not so awesome (percentagewise, few outdoorsmen get lost), for after all, the woods

are less dangerous than the modern highways. The priceless experience of canoe-camping in wild places should be relished without fear of harm, and being fully prepared, without worry of what might happen.

TRAIL BLAZES

Indians, explorers, mountain men, and pioneer trappers marked trails through the wilderness by blazing—using an ax, a sheath knife, or a machete at measured distances to hack out a chip from a tree. The exposed white surface under the bark, eye height, easily seen from a distance, gave the traveler a series of signs for proper trail progress. Use the blaze on limited or little-traveled portages and on unmarked wood trails which you know it will be necessary to retrace. In this day of shrinking wilderness, the extensive blazing of living trees, which can do harm, is discouraged. Blazes made by many wilderness campers can be confusing. If you must blaze, identify yours by making them at a height different from any previously cut.

The brush blaze is the simpler and preferred method. In an unknown stretch of the Berens River, in the company of an elderly Indian, we anxiously watched him blaze our trail. Because the river dropped precipitiously, a portage was in order, but at the water's edge, no marker or path was evident. Our guide walked confidently along, without slowing his stride, breaking branches on brush and trees with his fingers. The downward droop of numerous broken branches, shoulder height, broke the symmetry of orderly growth and were readily noticed. Soon, he found the shortest path between the take-out and the take-in points, and we proceeded with little delay.

While on their fur-trading trips in the northland, the Voyageurs practiced a form of landmark blaze—lobbing pines. On a prominent point visible for great distances against the skyline, they would select a tall pine tree. One would climb that tree, and with his ax "lob" off all the middle branches, leaving a full-blown crown and a tuft of natural foliage at the bottom. The shape of the tree was a peculiar, but eye-catching landmark. Lob pines, dating back to those fur-trading days, are reportedly still standing on Maypole Island in Rainy Lake, Canada.

HINDSIGHT

When traveling in new country, hindsight—regularly looking back to see the lay of the land you've just walked through—is an advantage when backtracking a route days or weeks later, for the woods, the landmarks, and the contours appear entirely different when viewed from the opposite direction. Your return trip will be much more safe and efficient if you've done this viewing.

SURVIVAL FOODS

Survival food abounds in its natural state in practically all of the canoe country. The combination of woods and waters offers a veritable supermart, enabling a person without regular food rations to survive in health for a long while. Resorting to the food of wild plants—living off the land—is for the lost or stranded, or when the grub rations are lost or exhausted. Meet the emergency by going to Nature's bountiful garden, pure and uncontaminated from DDT and scores of human handlers.

Among various cultures around the world and throughout history, food seems to have most diversity. Truly, "One man's meat is another man's poison," but in survival situations anywhere, food prejudices must be waved aside and life-sustaining potluck accepted: a handful of grubs or worms are as nourishing as a couple of hen's eggs; and lizards, locusts, crickets, grasshoppers, are prized as delicacies in many cultures.

SOME WILD EDIBLES, known by most outdoorsmen, are easily gathered in season: strawberries, raspberries, blackberries, gooseberries, blueberries, May apples, and currants. The less known—cowberries, bunch berries, and cloudberries—furnish supplements to a limited larder.

WILD FRUITS, such as grape, rum cherry, ground cherry, chokecherry, plums, and crab apples can be eaten as they are found, or boiled for jam. They are great thirst quenchers.

WILD GREENS, offer a source of vitamins. Gather stinging nettle leaves with the aid of leather gloves and a knife, and boil. Eat the tender young leaves of these plants as salads: sow thistle, lamb's quarters, ostrich fern, marsh marigold, chickweed, chicory, dandelion, shepherd's purse, plantain, and trillium. Later, when they begin to blossom, their toughness and their bitterness require them to be boiled. Not unlike them in taste, many of the wild greens belong to the spinach and the asparagus families.

Widespread in range and easily identified, *the willow tree* furnishes a food rich in vitamin C (much richer than oranges). The tender pith of young willow shoots, after peeling, can be eaten raw. The inner bark of the willow can be eaten raw after being exposed by removal of the outer bark, or scraped with a knife, dried and ground into a flour.

THE BARK OF THE WHITE BIRCH TREE (besides furnishing sheathing for the canoes of the Indians) also can serve as food, eaten raw, as the willow, or the inner bark dried and ground into flour for bread. Or, cut the inner bark into noodle-like strips to enrich stews and soups. Use birch bark only in emergencies, as the stripping of outer bark affects the beauty and health of the tree.

WILD ROOTS AND TUBERS. The hard tubers of the arrowhead plant, found along the edges of swamps, small ponds, or back-offs, look much like small potatoes. They grow at the ends of root runs in the mud, and you can harvest them simply by getting your feet wet and by digging. As inner bark, the flesh can be eaten raw, but becomes more palatable when baked, boiled, or roasted. Some outdoorsmen prefer arrowhead tubers to potatoes.

Wash and peel cattail roots very much as you do arrowhead roots. In spring, when the stalks are one to two feet high, they can be peeled like sugar cane and the pith eaten raw. This worldwide delicacy is known as "Cossack Asparagus."

WILD NUTS. Black walnut, butternut, hazelnut, hickory, and beechnut are very nutritious. Eat them immediately, pound into flour and bake into a nut bread, or save in their shells for future use. Often a close observation of squirrels and chipmunks will lead to nut sources.

THE SEEDS from various pine cones serve as edible, nutritious nut-like food.

BEVERAGES. The staghorn sumac, readily identifiable with its velvety branched twigs, resembling the horns of a deer, makes a delicious lemonade-type drink. Mash the small red berries, which grow in bunches like miniature grapes, then cover with boiling water and allow to steep. Remove the fine hairs by pouring through a screen or cloth. Enjoy this thirst quencher hot or cold.

SASSAFRAS TEA, famous since the days of Columbus as a spring tonic, is discussed in Chapter 5.

MAKE BIRCH TEA from the young twigs, tight leaves, and inner bark of the white birch tree, boil and steep into a spicy drink.

THE HEMLOCK TREE, widespread in canoe country, makes an aromatic and beneficial tea, rich in vitamin C. Place the young green tips (later in the year, the green needles) in a pot and pour boiling water over them. Strain through a cloth.

ALL CONIFER TREES furnish survival foods. As discussed above, preparation is the same —scrape off the inner bark and eat raw, boil or pound into a flour—to keep the body and soul together.

SNARE SMALL ANIMALS with nylon fishing line nooses placed along their runs. Richard Emiley, a boy of nine, in one of our parties, snared a snowshoe rabbit within an hour, on his first attempt. Rabbits and other nocturnal feeding animals follow definite paths, well-trod over the years, that are easily identified. To bring meat for the pot, place a few snares in strategic places. A rabbit, squirrel, chipmunk, porcupine, or muskrat is more readily captured than is a large animal.

BIRDS' EGGS offer another good source of wilderness food: after all, there's little nutritional difference between the eggs of crows, ducks, loons, and hens.

FRESH FISH is probably the best emergency food. Hooks, lures, and lines can be improvised, and netting, jacklighting, or spearing are acceptable when in dire circumstances. Frogs, crayfish, snails, clams, turtles, and snakes are fairly easy to find and to capture. They can be boiled or roasted over a bed of coals, or fried on a pan or hot stove.

In the situation of lost grub, or if there is danger of running out, start long before a serious food emergency develops: ration the regular food supply. Begin to augment the regular menu with wild edible foods. The gradual change will permit the digestive system to accommodate to less familiar foods.

Part Five

DISCIPLINE
FOR SAFETY

🌿 14 🌿

Common Sense
Along the
Trails

IN the wilderness, weather, wild waters, animals, and other aspects of environment are no threat to canoeists.

The only thing in the deep woods to fear is —yourself! Only you are a threat—in choosing a dangerous campsite, improperly using an ax, shooting a high-grade rapid, disregarding weather signs, planning inadequately for grub, carrying insufficient bedding, wearing inappropriate apparel, and wandering away from the campsite.

Practically every accident in the woods is avoidable, and each canoeist must learn the techniques of avoidance. You have to—the doctor is too far away.

In woods-and-water activities, you can: fracture a bone; upset a canoe and swallow a lot of water as you fall in; smash your canoe in the rapids; and get lost in trackless woods.

All these accidents are the disastrous results of one common cause—poor judgment. In reality, there's little to be afraid of in the wilderness milieu; you can keep out of trouble using a bit of common sense, without which you'll get into difficulty whether in the woods or elsewhere.

Habits of safety are acquired. Once the canoeist adopts the attitude of safety, which enhances the wilderness experience without interfering in any way with his sense of fun and freedom, with a complete sense of security he'll navigate difficult rivers, ride out heavy seas, and walk in the wilderness at night.

Don't Be Routed by Rising Rivers

The selection of a campsite and the stowing of canoes should be carefully considered and executed.

1. An index to a stream's high-water mark is indicated by driftwood and floating debris

125

One of many adequate and safe campsites along the Delta River in Alaska offering majestic mountain panoramas.

U.S. DEPT. OF THE INTERIOR: BUREAU OF LAND MANAGEMENT PHOTO

that can be seen lodged along the bank and in tree branches and shrubs. Heed them: camp and stow canoes above the high-water mark they indicate.

2. Should your trip be planned to canoe rivers that are harnessed by dams, be sure your campsite is far away enough from the high-water mark to prevent being washed away when the sluice gates are open.

3. Some small rivers (especially in the West) rise and fall quickly from rain that comes raging down the slopes from higher elevations.

4. To prevent the canoes from being washed away, be absolutely sure you always carry and stow them far enough from the water's indicated high-water mark.

Be Ready for Inclement Weather

In wet weather, with proper rain gear and adequate tarp protection of duffle, it is often possible to continue a forward course, but when a protracted siege of heavy rain occurs, it becomes necessary to hole up for the duration.

Rain need not spoil the fun of wilderness camping. Some suggestions to assure its minimal effect are:

1. Pitch a fly, made of waterproof tenting, in front of the tent, as an extension of the roof line, to make an adequate front porch. In this way:

A. The fly provides a sheltered area;

B. The front door of the tent is protected; and

C. The crowding inside the tent is eased.

The fly (tarp) should measure at least six by eight feet, and can be as large as ten by fourteen feet (depending on logistics). Because it weighs less than four pounds, the smaller size is not burdensome, and in fair weather it also can serve as a pack cloth, ground, or protective covering.

The tarp should have grommets at each corner and fairly large cords attached, so that it can be pitched with a minimum of poles.

2. Build and maintain a fire on the protected area under the fly:

A. As a safety measure, keep the fire small;

B. Use this fire for cooking and for drying damp clothing;

C. Allow the heat to drift back into the tent to eliminate dampness there; and

D. To help keep your sleeping gear dry, which it is important to do at all times, as discussed earlier in the book.

Enjoy Wet Weather

With compatible companions, neither inclement weather nor rain need be disheartening. Being tent-bound by weather, it is possible to spend an enjoyable and stimulating day discussing the joys of the world (if not its woes), patching and mending gear and clothes, scouring pots and pans, whipping up a cake batter, reading and writing.

The wilderness canoeist is thoroughly prepared for rain, even though it may not come.

River flow at West River, Jamaica, Vermont, is controlled by Ball Mountain Dam, constructed, operated, and maintained by New England Division, U.S. Army Corps of Engineers. By prior arrangement with canoeist, damkeeper releases exact volume of water to afford maximum use of river below impoundment.
CORPS OF ENGINEERS: U.S. ARMY

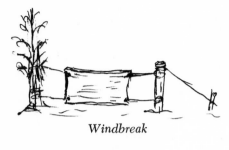

Windbreak

Locked in frame: Can be used in many ways

Wood shelter

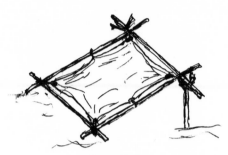

Gear shelter

Hasty tent

Emergency signal (afloat or on dry land)

TARP TRICKS

If it does, you won't be "rained out," and you'll come to accept inclement weather in the pattern of happy out-of-doors days.

In the quest of making the wet wilderness into a comfortable home, you will become wet and fatigued, but in the absence of contaminating germs, there is rarely a cold the next morning.

The Wind-Chill Factor

Today, in their daily weather reports forecasters are indicating the wind-chill factor along with temperatures, which of themselves are no indication of the chilling factor. The wind speed accompanying the temperature

Wind Speed MPH	Actual thermometer reading				
	20°	30°	40°	50°	
0	20	30	40	50	
10	4	16	28	40	Wind
20	—10	4	18	32	chill
30	—18	—2	13	28	equivalent
40	—21	—6	10	26	

DISCOMFITURE INDEX

indicates a wind-chill reading—also called "the discomfiture index."

The chart values indicate that wind, even when the actual temperature is mild, steals the body's heat, and when combined with low temperatures, it can become downright uncomfortable. The retention of generated heat enables a body to operate efficiently.

To combat coldness:

1. Make sure you get plenty of food for the body to transform to heat;

2. Chopping wood, hiking, paddling, and swinging the arms also help; and

3. Of prime importance is the proper clothing to help retain generated heat.

This retention is abetted by the layer method of dressing—adding clothing when cold, taking off when hot—which includes: net underwear, allowing air to circulate at skin level and to filter out through neck, wrist, and pant-cuff openings; next a layer of loose clothing, such as wool or synthetic shirt and pants, which retain warmth when wet; then insulation clothes in the form of coat or sweater; finally, a water-and-wind repellent outer shell—jacket, rain gear, or poncho.

Protection Against the Sun

Extended exposure to the sun is dangerous to some people. The human epidermis is a microscopically thin covering consisting of five layers, the innermost layer containing basal cells which produce granules of brownish pigment (tan) called "melanin." The degree of tan one can acquire is determined by the quantity of melanin that the basal cells are capable of producing. Persons having less melanin run the risk of dangerous over-exposure.

The nose, forehead, lips, ears, neck, and the back of hands are especially vulnerable to sun because they have little flesh beneath the epidermis and cannot tolerate sunburn as can other parts of the body.

Water, rocks, and sand serve as reflective agents which can compound the sun's harmful rays. It also has been ascertained that even mild exposure can cause serious damage when antibiotics, tranquilizers, sulpha drugs, and antihistamines are taken, the power of these drugs being multiplied many times over when the person who has any one of them in his system is exposed to bright sunshine.

Harmful rays of the sun can be blocked out in many ways: by wearing hats, caps, long-sleeved shirts, face masks, nose guards, and with the application of petrolatum, oil, lard, zinc oxide, talcum powder, and many other commercial preparations. The most effective sun screens are paramino-benzoic acid and newer benzophenone compounds, which the tubes will indicate.

Even on the hottest day, the wilderness canoeist wears a large floppy hat with wide brim, long-sleeved shirt, and full-length trousers. Without such protection, exposure to sun should be limited to short periods of time.

Tanning Before the Trip

Some canoeists plan to tan before going on the trip and observe these principles whenever in the sun:

1. This preparation for a wilderness trip cannot be hurried.

2. Exposure to sun after three-thirty (Day-

Parents and children are comfortable with proper clothing to help retain generated heat. Note the man's life jacket and the children's bib and horse-collar life preservers.

MICHIGAN TOURIST COUNCIL PHOTO

light Saving Time) will tan the body instead of burning it.

3. Gradual tanning is best achieved by limiting your first days' exposure during the hottest part of the day to ten minutes— usually 10:30 A.M. to 2:30 P.M.

4. Soon the exposed parts of the body become tanned to a point where you can take the sun longer and more easily.

5. It takes two weeks of gradual exposure to the sun to develop the kind of tan indicated in some magazine ads.

Water Intake

During warm daylight hours, there is a great body-fluid loss in strenuous activity. Sunshine, dry air, and wind make it necessary to keep plenty of water in your system.

Fatigue may be caused by body dehydration, so drink plenty of water, and often!

There is little chance of drinking more liquids than you need. The real danger is in not drinking enough.

Wear a Life Preserver

Jackets with excellent built-in flotation, having the appearance and the warmth of good, insulated garments, are becoming popular among canoeists. The buoyant vest, as well as being neater, lighter, and less bulky than jacket-style life preservers, is comfortable to wear and permits freedom of arm movement.

Another ideal life preserver is the newer, horse-collar or bib style that fits snugly around the neck and secures around the chest and waist with ties and straps. The horse-collar preserver is best for holding a person's head above water; poor swimmers feel confident with them.

A preserver that keeps the head above water is vital, as the best swimmer can be knocked unconscious in a fall from the canoe

The sensible canoeist, solo or tandem, always wears a life preserver, this one being the bib and horse-collar style.
MINNESOTA CONSERVATION DEPT. PHOTO

—especially in white water. Also, in cold water (40 to 50 degrees), a swimmer will lose consciousness in less than an hour, and the danger is there—expert swimmer or not.

The Water Rescue

When a person is struggling in the water, there are many emergency measures that even rescuers who are non-swimmers can use:

1. Throw out to the struggler any floating object—a long, sealed tin can or a tightly rolled sleeping bag.

2. If the struggler is near, reach out an arm or a leg, or extend the reach by using a shirt, trousers, or a rope for him to grasp.

3. One method of providing flotation is to invert a metal or canvas water bucket or large pot, so that the air is trapped inside. If the person in the water will rest his chin on the edge of an empty bucket or pot (open side up), he will be aided in flotation.

4. Either the person in the water or the rescuer can take off his trousers, tie a knot in each pant-leg cuff or bottom, and blow air into both trouser legs while the trousers are inverted in the water. The legs will balloon out with the trapped air and float a person for hours.

5. Air blown into the pockets of trousers gives enough buoyancy in an emergency.

6. Remember, the body is buoyant—and relaxed, easy motions in water abet that buoyancy.

Treatment After the Rescue

An important part of any rescue comes after the rescued has been "saved." In terms of shock and of heart strain, the aftermath of a rescue can be as damaging as the accident for all concerned—the rescued and the rescuer or rescuers.

1. Even though the rescued person(s) ap-

pears to be, and insists that, he's "all right," treat him for shock.

2. Don't fail to tend to the rescuer(s): treat them, too, for shock: some have collapsed from exhaustion after a save, even though they appeared to have suffered no adverse effects and felt none immediately after the rescue.

The Foolish Dare

An exuberant crew member, confident of his swimming ability, is ever ready to respond to a challenge—perhaps the challenge of being able to swim to a distant island or to the shore.

In all such attempts, the canoe should accompany or convoy the swimmer.

Always keep in mind, it's often the expert swimmer who gets into trouble—by overestimating his strength and his ability in the particular situation, especially when he is not completely familiar with the water.

The Dangers and Hazards of Fire

At all times, when an outboard motor is part of the gear of a trip, be careful of spilled gasoline that accumulates on the floor or in the bottom of the canoe. Tragedies from such situations have occurred when a smoker accidentally ignited the fuel.

To begin with, a canoe should not be overburdened with a large outboard motor, and the freeboard standards should be observed to prevent shipping water in high waves or when suddenly making a turn.

A Final Caution for Smokers

Take care if you smoke:

1. Stop!

2. Sit down and relax.

3. Use a flat rock as your ask tray, or dig down to mineral soil with your heel.

4. Crush out your smoke before you move on.

The number of human lives, the acres of timber, and the property loss from forest fires can be assessed, but many other losses cannot be—the death of birds, animals, and fish.

The restoration of flora and fauna is a very slow process. Every forest fire, no matter how small, disturbs the natural and vital relationship (ecology) of woods, soil, water, animal, bird, and fish life—and ultimately man's welfare.

First Aid

The administration of first aid, like everything else, has changed in recent times.

First aid for arterial bleeding, for snake bite, burns, asphyxiation, infections, etc., has changed so much, that an old first-aid manual is outdated.

The use of a tourniquet, of artificial respiration, the treatment for burns, the method of bandaging, and the use of antiseptics are but a few areas that have been improved or altered.

As first-aid procedures have changed considerably in the light of recent discoveries and research, wilderness canoeists (certainly one of the crew) should be well versed in the new techniques as taught by the American Red Cross.

The average wilderness camper does not know that the treatment for sunstroke is almost opposite that of heat exhaustion, and the difference should be known.

First-Aid Kits

First-aid kits are numerous, but the crew member in charge of first aid probably will wish to stock his own kit.

The contents should include, first of all, the personal medicines that have been prescribed by doctors for the members of the crew.

From there, items should include: gauze pads, bandages, and Band-aids; pain killers, laxatives; medicines for diarrhea; toothache drops; cold tablets; topical antiseptic; Halzone tablets and iodine for water purification; salt tablets; aspirin; skin-soothing medications; antihistamine; and snake-bite kit (if in snake-infested territory).

Instruments include: a thermometer, forceps, surgical scissors, and razor blades.

Such items as cotton swabs, alcohol, triangular bandage, first-aid spray, iodine or mercurochrome for application.

Other items, naturally, may be added in making up the wilderness emergency kit, as well as the hope that you'll not have to use most of them.

S.O.S. in the Extreme Emergency

Should that extreme emergency overtake your crew in the deep wilderness (in approximately one thousand miles of bush canoe travel, I have never encountered it), the veterans of the hinterland inform me that the best way to get immediate help in a remote area is to set a huge bonfire on a small island.

The forests are being watched constantly for smoke.

A bush plane will soon be dropping in to investigate.

✤ 15 ✤

Animals— Friends and Foes

ANIMALS in the wilderness, from the smallest mouse to the huge moose, must be considered, but without any overtones of threat that might lessen the ardor of crew members intent on meeting them near their haunts.

Your consideration of wild animals should take a middle course—between extreme confidence in feeling that no animal will harm you if you do not act as a threat and of being afraid of every animal in the wilderness. Common sense principles of dealing with some of them that you are apt to meet are helpful.

The Black Bear

In some wilderness canoeing areas, the black bear can be especially bothersome. Because bears are lazy—as you and I—instead of scrounging for food, they readily gravitate to man's domain for the easy meal.

In some canoeing areas where bears have learned that tin cans carry food, they are known to play havoc with your supplies.

The black bear usually returns to a campsite where he has previously found food.

This camp wrecker's behavior is prompted neither by animosity toward, nor hatred of, people, but by a combination of curiosity and hunger. Sweet and salty foods (bacon, for instance) drive the black bear to ripping and to chewing everything in sight.

In black-bear infested country, it is best to camp on small islands, where there is an inadequate supply of natural food for bears and a restricted prowl area.

When taking precautions in the wilderness, remember, the black bears have poor vision; to find food, they rely almost entirely on their sense of smell.

The logical measure, then, is for the camper to prevent the aroma of food from being borne on the air. Store meat, bacon, fish, cheese,

135

aromas wafting to the free-loading, hungry bears.

A Bear Alarm

A frequently used alarm system is made by storing food under the inverted canoe and placing pots and pans on top. The clang of dislodged pots generally indicates the presence of a black bear.

Loud noises, bright flashlight beams, poking up the fire, and yelling usually rout the intruder. Sometimes, old, experienced bears will not move, and the crew will have to decide to move camp to the small island campsite.

Never Feed Bears

The feeding of black bears by campers leads to some disastrous results. In Yellowstone Park, although there are many warnings posted advising visitors NOT to feed the bears, involving them since 1930 have been 1,825 personal injuries and 5,081 cases of property damage to tents, food packs, automobiles, etc.

In practically every instance, sloppy camping habits and the illegal feeding of bears were responsible for the personal injuries and the property damage.

The black bear has capable claws and teeth, but neither looks for a fight nor attacks man without provocation; he battles only when he is completely cornered, when he has no escape route, or when protecting cubs.

The Grizzly Bear

The grizzly bear (appropriately named, in Latin, *Ursus Horribilis*), fortunately is not too common in wilderness canoeing areas.

During the summer of 1967, the nation was shocked when, in Montana's Glacier National

Black bear.
E. P. HADDON PHOTO; U.S. BUREAU OF SPORT FISHERIES & WILDLIFE

butter, etc., in plastic bags or friction-top cans —under water if necessary.

Should you plan to leave your campsite unattended for a while, hang up the food (enclosed in a plastic bag) from a branch at least twelve feet high, on a tree too small to support the weight of a bear. Throw the rope over a branch, haul up the bag, and tie it in a place inaccessible to the bear.

Or, string a rope between two saplings and suspend the food bag between them out of reach of a bear.

Never store food in a tent; bears are known to tear canvas walls when their olfactory radar registers food. Food scraps and used tin cans must be properly burned as a part of the kitchen-cleaning chore. Burying garbage is another precaution. Also, washing dishes immediately after each meal tends to cut down

Park, two nineteen-year-old coeds were mauled to death by grizzly bears. The tragedies led to an extensive grizzly bear research program in all Rocky Mountain and Alaskan parks.

Now, each camper entering back country is furnished a large plastic sack for carrying out empty cans, bottles, and other food containers. All persons are required to bring out all unburnable items.

The grizzly, being an intelligent animal, learns quickly to associate the smell of the presence of humans with food for themselves, and their natural shyness turns to boldness as they come to depend on easy food sources left by careless campers.

The grizzly bear research is the basis for the following suggestions:

1. Never hike alone in bear country.

2. Detour around areas where there are evidences of bear, or wait until the bear moves away from your route.

3. Make noises by wearing bells or other noisemakers, such as a whistle, or by loud talking.

4. If suddenly face to face with a grizzly bear, remain calm and do not move.

5. If the bear rears up, speak in a soft, steady monotone to reassure the animal.

6. Climb a tree if a grizzly is nearby, because only young grizzlies can climb. An old-timer's humorous definition of the difference between a black bear and a grizzly bear is:

"If you kick a black bear, he will climb a
    tree;
"If you kick a grizzly, you'll climb the
    tree."

7. Make your presence known to the bear, and if you see one in the distance, keep upwind so that your scent will announce your presence and you won't take him by surprise.

8. Don't run away from a bear; your flight will excite the animal and suggest that he

Grizzly bear with cubs.
U.S. BUREAU OF SPORT FISHERIES & WILDLIFE

chase you. It will be impossible to outdistance him. On the whole, bears (like most animals) are usually anxious to give man a wide berth.

9. Don't get on a rise above a bear; bears do not like other animals above them. Uphill is a bear's normal escape route.

10. Never harass a bear unless it is actually, physically attacking someone, and then try to distract it by shouting or throwing sticks or stones.

11. Be very wary when berry-picking, as bears, too, like berries, and in season often are gleaning the wild fruit.

Finally—

A morbid precaution. As the rare fatalities from attacking grizzlies come from their biting humans in the back of the neck, or from their disemboweling them, the best defense is to lie down, fold up into a tight ball, with hands clasped behind the neck. Pull the knees up under the chin to protect your stomach. In this position, lie perfectly still—which, obviously, may be quite difficult.

At best, animal behavior cannot be predicted. Many circus performers have discovered that, after many years of control, animals turn on them to inflict serious injury.

The Porcupine

The slow-moving porcupine is a gnawing menace; it plays havoc with equipment by chewing anything that contains salt.

The perspiration that permeates canoe paddles, gunwales, ax handles, hats, shoes, pack straps, etc., is a source of salt that the porkie relishes. I have seen trappers' cabin doors completely gnawed away along the edges, where their hands had pushed them shut.

In porcupine country, any gear that is salted by sweaty hands should be secured or hung out of their reach. The porky has a short memory, and when stoned and driven from camp, seems to forgive, and without grudge, comes lumbering back.

Porcupine.
L. K. GOUCH PHOTO; U.S. BUREAU OF SPORT FISHERIES & WILDLIFE

The slow-moving porcupine, of course, cannot shoot his quills, but the high-speed swishing of his tail can drive quills deep into your leg. As a last resort, pesky porcupines can be killed easily with a long club. One reason for their protective status is that for starving hinterland travelers, they offer a source of survival meat.

When disposing of a killed porcupine, never try to pick up a "dead" porky until you're sure he is DEAD: and even then only by a paw, and with great care.

Antlered Animals

Deer, moose, and elk seldom enter a wilderness camping area, but occasionally during the night, one of them gets curious and comes close enough to become entangled in a clothes line or tent guy rope.

Many times, in favorable food and cover areas, the moose comes lumbering into camp to investigate your quarters. This bovine-like creature, though huge, is quite docile, and in the summertime rarely causes trouble. The size of the largest animal on the North American continent gives rise to fictitious ferocity, which of course is not typical—occurring mostly during the rutting or calf-raising season.

If your campsite is not hemmed in by boulders, brush, and clothes lines, an easy exit for curious animals is afforded, and a little noise sends them scooting away. Patience and caution are the watchwords, as it may take a little time for the animal intruder to decide to leave.

Raccoons and Skunks

The clean, friendly raccoons are a pleasure to watch as they come nosing about the campsite after dark looking for scraps of food.

They are very clever at opening bags and

boxes, and seem to untie pack straps and knots that would baffle an old salt.

Though generally shy and taking off when shooed, the coon can become a real fighter when cornered or injured.

The skunk, a docile animal, is completely harmless when not endangered and when given a wide berth. I have enjoyed many along the woodland trails without one unpleasant experience. After a reconnaissance of a campsite, they leave—sometimes with the prodding of a flashlight to hasten their departure.

The skunk expels his fumigant only when frightened or endangered, always giving a warning with a stamping of the feet or an arching of its back as it brings around the business end in an aiming movement. Sometimes he actually performs a front-paw hand stand for the same reason.

A clean camp discourages raccoons and skunks.

Chipmunks, Mice, and Squirrels

All of the small rodents seem to drop in for a visit when nuts, cereals, or candy bars are available.

The chipmunks, mice, voles, and lemmings neither play havoc with a grub supply nor endanger safety, but the sanitary aspects and the safeguarding of rations require food to be inaccessible to them.

Various kinds of squirrels are most certain to visit your campsite, but as with all other furry and friendly visitors, a word of caution about feeding them is in order. They may be covered with fleas, lice, or other parasites carrying dangerous diseases.

Never make pets of them by trying to touch or to pet them, as a nip on the fingers may be dangerous. Because the rabies virus is carried in the saliva of squirrels and other animals, and they clean their paws and nails with their

teeth, a bite or skin puncture, even from a scratch, may transfer the rabies to you, requiring a painful series of shots, and a delay in their administration can be fatal.

J. MALCOLM GREANY PHOTO; U.S. BUREAU OF SPORT FISHERIES & WILDLIFE

E. P. HADDON PHOTO; U.S. BUREAU OF SPORT FISHERIES & WILDLIFE

Antlered animals: A. Moose; B. Mule deer bucks.

Raccoon.
C. J. HENRY PHOTO; U.S. BUREAU OF SPORT
FISHERIES & WILDLIFE

Poisonous Snakes

In northern wilderness canoe country, the chances of being endangered by a poisonous snake are very remote; and even in southern climes, where they are prevalent, the fatalities are practically nil. As with other animals, when in snake country, make a lot of noise, as snakes avoid humans whenever they can, and rarely will you find one near a campsite.

Don't poke your hands into holes among rocks or in logs, or under stumps. Snakes rarely enter a tent with a sewed-in floor, but sleeping on the ground in a sleeping bag is another matter.

For snake country, the jungle hammock is recommended. There are only four kinds of poisonous snakes in America—the rattler, the copperhead, the water moccasin, and the coral snake—and they are rarely found in wilderness canoeing areas—except, of course, in the Southern states.

REX GARY SCHMIDT PHOTO; U.S. BUREAU OF SPORT
FISHERIES & WILDLIFE

E. R. KALMBACH PHOTO; U.S. BUREAU OF SPORT
FISHERIES & WILDLIFE

*Poisonous snakes in the south: A. Ground rattler in vicinity of Great Bend, Kansas;
B. Water moccasin, near Gueydan, Louisiana.*

Part Six

※ ※ ※

SOURCES OF INFORMATION AND MAPS ON WILDERNESS LOCALES

※ ※ ※

16

The Canadian Wilderness

THE wilderness canoe trip holds endless possibilities, and Canada's network of rivers and lakes provides an unlimited choice of routes.

The remarkable system of water trails which makes Canada preeminently the country of the canoeist affords a great variety of trips; days, weeks, and months can be spent on a single cruise, or one may journey by train, by steamer, or by bush plane to remote waters, and in the immediate vicinity of the drop-off point use his allotted time paddling, fishing, and exploring.

In the northern hinterland, the waters and the land are the same today as when traveled by Voyageurs of the Hudson's Bay Company and the North West Company more than two hundred years ago. A canoe trip over these routes becomes, in one way, modern man's response to one of the last few challenges to the pioneer spirit.

There are thousands of far-flung wilderness waters in Canada and the United States yet to be discovered. With no claim to completeness, a few highlights are included in this book, the fragmentary list mentioning waters for their inspirational value—a nudge to stimulate the flow of adrenalin in the adventure-seeking wilderness canoeists. The provinces are considered from west to east.

YUKON

The Yukon is a land of broad dimensions—high mountains, big game fish, and sporty rivers—its modern frontier life retaining the flavor of 1896 when the Bard of the North, Robert Service, described the scene of the world's most spectacular gold rush in the land of the Midnight Sun.

Yukon's challenging miles of navigable

143

Wilderness canoeing is popular in British Columbia.
TRAILCRAFT CANOE CO. PHOTOS

wilderness rivers await rediscovery time and again by modern canoeists. The Yukon and its tributaries (such as the Yukon lakes) can be termed navigable for canoes. The river currents vary between two and five miles per hour, and all provide excellent downhill runs. Although on Yukon's waterways there's an absence of "death defying" aspects, the independent canoeist (the one without a guide) must understand his craft in relation to the type of water upon which he embarks. Practically all routes lead through uninhabited wilderness, requiring complete self-sufficiency.

Canoeists who expect to make extended trips must notify the Royal Canadian Mounted Police post nearest their point of departure and satisfy authorities that their equipment is adequate. Guides are available.

A reliable source of wilderness information: Yukon Wilderness Unlimited, P.O. Box 1126, Whitehorse, Yukon, Canada. Another: The Yukon Department of Travel and Information, P.O. Box 2703, Whitehorse, Yukon Territory, Canada.

NORTHWEST TERRITORIES

A highway to adventure is the mighty Mackenzie River, navigable for more than one thousand miles, flowing north from Great Slave Lake to the Beaufort Sea—a five-mile-wide giant replete with innumerable islands, feeder streams of every size and description, which, after leaving their northland jungles, pour their strengthening contributions into the Mackenzie. Since the time of the Voyageurs, the Mackenzie route has been a major highway to Arctic waters.

Cruising this vast watershed, the canoeist becomes acquainted with forces greater than himself—the Eskimo and the Indian cultures, the white man's struggle in an alien land, and the importance of a mighty river to the life of the land and to its people.

Source of information for canoeists: Travel-Arctic, Tourist Development Section (TB), Yellowknife, Northwest Territories, Canada; and Bureau of Land, Parks, Forests, Ottawa, Ontario, Canada.

BRITISH COLUMBIA

Within the boundaries of British Columbia are thousands of square miles of provincial land for wilderness canoers and campers. There are waters where the paddle of the white man has yet not been dipped. One hears of these from chance words of the Indians, and even they cannot fully satisfy curiosity regarding them.

In Tweedmuir Park, one may embark on the "Grand Circle" route, traversing Ootsa, Whitesail, Eutsuk, and Tetachuk Lakes, gaze in wonder at snow-capped mountains, glaciers, and heavily forested areas.

Another interesting trip takes the canoeist down the Peace River (beginning at Summit Lake) through the heart of the Rockies to Rocky Mountain Canyon, where a portage of fourteen miles by vehicle is made to Hudson Hope.

The dimensions of British Columbia are tremendous, and canoe trips of one hundred, two hundred, and five hundred miles are possible—to challenge the most avid adventurer.

For information, contact: Department of Travel Industry, (TB), Victoria, British Columbia, Canada.

ALBERTA

An example of Alberta's wilderness is Jasper National Park, remaining little changed from the day when fur trader, explorer David Thompson found it in 1811. It is one of the unspoiled areas in North America. The paddler who launches his canoe at Jasper and points its bow downstream has before him an adventure trail that ends at Aklavik, far beyond the Arctic Circle.

The rugged topography of Alberta's north keeps the canoeist mostly on the numerous hinterland lakes, exceptions being the canoeable waters of the Miette and Malignes rivers. White water enthusiasts (in kayaks) race with the currents of the Athabasca River from Athabasca Falls to Jasper. The water is fast and white, not recommended for canoes, making it a rousing trip to the take-out below Old Fort Point bridge on the right bank.

For downright distance and endurance, demanding raw courage and a lot of experience, the combination of cruising the Peace, the Slave, and the Mackenzie rivers makes possible routes running into hundreds of miles.

For information, write: Alberta Government Travel Bureau, 1629 Centennial Building, Edmonton 15, Alberta, Canada.

SASKATCHEWAN

The Saskatchewan River, which in Cree Indian language means "The river that flows swiftly," became the main route of the early fur traders and provided a vital east-west water highway wholly within Canada. Henry Kelsey, of the Hudson's Bay Company, was the first white man to lay eyes on the Saskatchewan River, in 1691, while on a prodigious journey from York Factory. He was the first white man to view the great western Canadian prairies.

In experiencing the rivers of Saskatchewan, you also will be adding to the tradition of 1772, when Joseph Frobisher, fur trader and explorer, penetrated the area and laid the groundwork for the opening up of this tremendous area of Canada's northwest.

The Churchill River trip from Île-a-la-Crosse to the bridge at Otter Rapids remains today a wilderness river where moose still frequent its shores, and deeply worn portage trails, campsites, and an occasional cabin bear witness to the canoeists who, over the centuries, have passed that way.

Traveling the waterways of Saskatchewan, the modern-day canoeist feels the faint memory of the early fur trade rivalry between the Hudson's Bay Company and the North West Company, of Crees camped on its shores, the annual spectacular of migratory geese and ducks, and solitude everywhere.

Saskatchewan's wilderness canoe country lies deep in its little-known, sparsely populated, northern half—far beyond the road's end. There are many wilderness trip possibilities, all of them offering a rich heritage of Indian-lore past and present, history, wilderness scenery, and excellent fishing. The Churchill River watershed is a highway that opens up the country. Twenty-six canoe trips through wilderness areas are listed, with mileage, portages, and days of travel. Details available from: Information Branch, Department of Natural Resources, Government Administration Building, Regina, Saskatchewan, Canada. The Tourist Development Branch, Saskatchewan Industry Department, has an office in the Power Building, Regina, Saskatchewan, Canada.

MANITOBA

The thrill of casting a fishing lure into the mystic waters of an unfished lake or stream is possible in the remote waters of Manitoba. The wilderness canoeist, in most cases, is first an explorer, second a fisherman, but in Manitoba there is ample opportunity to be both.

Bush plane travel is the magic carpet that, within an hour or so, can waft the canoeist from civilization to the mirror stillness of many wilderness waters. A look at the map of Manitoba reveals rivers such as the Pigeon, Setting, Paint, Manigotagan, Wanipigow, Echamimish, Athapapuskow, Wekusko, and hundreds of others, which, by their very names and strangeness, reveal wilderness waters in the truest sense.

A swamp in the wilderness also can evoke an awe-inspiring observation for the canoeist who is willing to travel in out-of-the-way places, such as this excerpt from the daily log of a paddler on the Kautunigan route, crossing the Broadleaf, Cammon, Bloodvein, Berens rivers and numerous lakes from Wallace Lake to the settlement of Berens Reviers:

> "This, as the last swamp, is really a new world. The river is wide, shallow, and easy-flowing. Absolute silence hangs over the miles of empty wilderness. What a change from the violent tumultuous roar of rapids and falls.
>
> "In the last glows of the sunset, and through the quiet moonlight, beavers can be seen rippling their way to and from a low hut at the mouth of the creek.
>
> "Early in the morning, the fog, tinted with a somewhat savage odor, rises slowly as an incense to its creator."

For further information, write: Department of Tourism and Recreation, Parks Branch, 809 Norquay Building, 401 York Avenue, Winnipeg, Manitoba, Canada.

ONTARIO

With its 250,000 lakes and connecting rivers, Ontario offers a lifetime of canoeing. It encompasses over a thousand miles from the eastern Rideau Lake District to the Lake of the Woods at its western boundary. The hinterland of Ontario lies farther south than in any other Canadian province, requiring less travel distance for wilderness experiences to Mid-western stateside canoeists.

The wilderness possibilities in Ontario are legion, and canoeists increase greatly with each passing year. So extensive are the canoeable waters that the province officials find it impossible to keep current on use, needs, and future plans.

Jewels in Ontario's sparkling necklace of clear lakes include the canoeing treasury of Quetico, Algonquin, and Algoma.

QUETICO PROVINCIAL PARK, since 1913, has been set apart as a "forest reserve, fish and game preserve" and canoe country without peer. Quetico, with an area of 1,750 square miles, is primarily a wilderness area for canoeists, and is protected against any disturbance which might cause the deterioration and destruction of the wilderness environment.

Canoeing is synonymous with the Quetico, dating back to its early inhabitants, who painted in red pigment bird and animal figures on the rock faces over the water. They can still be seen today. The artists are unknown, but the mystery adds a certain aura to a canoe trip on these ancient trails. Canoe trips may be planned for any length of time from a few days to more than a month. True wilderness is found beyond the two-day trip. A booklet, *Canoe Routes of Quetico Provincial Park*, describes routes, equipment, supplies, and points of entry.

Outfitters are located near the entrance to Quetico, but canoeists who have their own equipment and supplies need only a travel permit, on which they must state the route intended, and the time to cover it. The permit serves as a safety measure, in that it informs authorities of the whereabouts of wilderness canoeists in case of emergency, and also acts as a control during periods of high fire hazard.

Access to Quetico Provincial Park's main entrance is on Highway 11, at Dawson Trail on French Lake, one hundred miles west of the Lakehead Cities of Port Arthur and Fort William. For additional information concerning Quetico, contact the Park Superintendent, Quetico Provincial Park, Department of Lands and Forest, Atikokan, Ontario, Canada, or the District Forester, Department of Lands and Forests, Fort Francis, Ontario, Canada.

ALGONQUIN PROVINCIAL PARK, in eastern Ontario, is more convenient to Eastern stateside canoeists. Similar to Quetico in its potential for wilderness retreat, the sanctuary is virtually unscarred by roads, as Highway 60 cuts through its lower portion, barely scratching the three-thousand square-mile surface of this vast wilderness. In order to enjoy Algonquin's wilderness, fish the bountiful interior lakes, and observe the virgin forests, the sportsman must participate in the full experience of canoe-camping. Firearms are barred from the park since the days—sixty years ago—when rangers battled poachers with fists, rifle butts, and canoe paddles, to win this sanctuary.

Outfitters are on hand for partial or complete outfitting, for comprehensive instruction detailing route, portages, campsites, and pinpointing productive fishing waters. You will also be informed that it is possible to take a canoe trip of more than seventy miles and never encounter a portage of more than one-half mile. The park is open from April to October, and July and August generally are considered the best months except for those who prefer the spring blooms and fall colors. There has never been a fatality in Algonquin, and one reassuring safety measure is the aircraft patrol that covers the park daily, and can be signaled if an emergency arises. Any questions? Write the park superintendent.

ALGOMA DISTRICT OF THE PROVINCE OF ONTARIO, comprising over sixteen thousand square miles, and lying along the north shore of Lakes Superior and Huron, just above the state of Michigan, is roadless, but is made available to the wilderness canoeist by a unique railroad, the Algoma Central. It is one of Canada's most interesting railroads. The ACR has been running since the days when the lumberjacks, trappers, and miners outnumbered the fishermen and canoeists. In its 289 miles (mostly wilderness), the railway climbs, curves, dips, puffing up small mountains, across high trestles, among spruce swamps, and through dry pine plains dotted with lakes. Camera buffs will especially be interested in Agawa Canyon, a rocky defile coming alive with cascading waterfalls and white water splashing on the canyon floor.

The novelty of the railroad by itself is an experience, a frontier train puffing toward wild country, carrying miners, missionaries, prospectors, fishermen, and canoeists. At mealtime there are no frills in the diner, no tablecloths, no menu, no steward, but everything is neat and clean, and there's a good cook in the galley.

The train leaves Sault Ste. Marie at 7 A.M. daily, and your car is safe in the railroad parking lot until you return. Don't worry about the confusion at the station, men and women milling about canoes and piles of equipment. The railway employees will load all baggage before departure, and soon you'll be beyond the fringe—ready to be dropped off, hours later, anywhere along the route you choose. The canoe and gear are unloaded, the canoe carried to the river's edge, the gear and food stowed, and you're ready to consider beaver lodges, otter slides down steep slopes, abandoned gold mines, and trout on the way down to civilization. Recommended canoe trips include: Michipicoten River, two to three days through wild country, but there are not too many portages, nor white water.

Batchawana River from Mile 80 to Lake Superior. A rather rough, but scenic five-day trip.

Sand River from Mile 138 to Lake Superior offers excellent trout fishing along the rough route that requires twenty-eight portages. Seven days.

Montreal River from Chapleau on the Canadian Pacific Railway (153 miles north of Thessalon) to mile 92 on the Algoma Central, or continue by canoe to Lake Superior. Ten to twelve days.

Algoma information may be obtained from Traffic Manager, Algoma Central Railway, Sault Ste. Marie, Ontario, Canada.

QUEBEC

The historic St. Lawrence River is Canada's oldest highway. Many lovely valleys approach it from the north and the south: the Saguenay, guarded by precipitous cliffs; the St. Maurice, where a famous canoe race from La Tuque to Trois Rivières is held; the Richelieu, with its historic forts; the Charlevoix district in quiet, pastoral beauty that has long been beloved of artists and photographers. So much of canoeing history is tied up with the St. Lawrence, that avid canoeists should experience some sector of it. North of the St. Lawrence, in the forest fastness, dwell the French Canadians, whose ancestors typify best the famous Voyageurs. Many wilderness trips can be made from the transcontinental line of the Canadian National Railway. Bourmont is the starting point for the Kapitachuan River route to Maniwaki. Another trip starts near Parent from Menjobagus Lake, crosses a height of land to the Mitchinamekus River and follows that stream down to the Lievre River and on to Mont Laurier. Quebec is, in great part, a rugged province of varying altitude, mostly forested, traversed by innumerable rivers, and holding hundreds of lakes of all sizes.

The parks of Quebec cover some fifty-five thousand square miles; the Park Service has worked out some itineraries for canoeists, and a leaflet describing them is available on request.

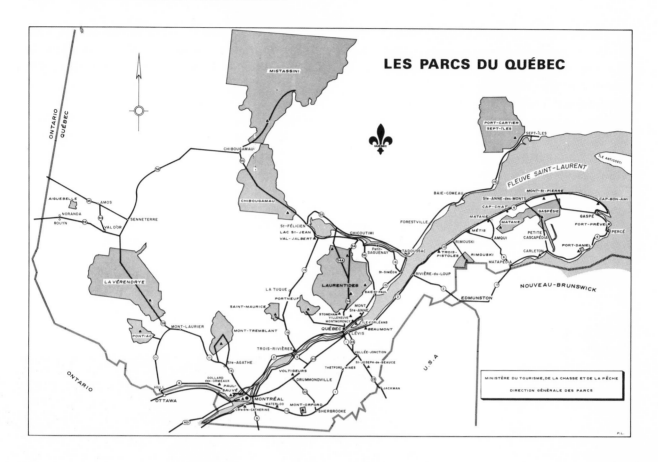

LES PARCS DU QUÉBEC

MINISTÈRE DU TOURISME, DE LA CHASSE ET DE LA PÊCHE
DIRECTION GÉNÉRALE DES PARCS

Getting ready to launch a canoe for a wilderness canoe-camping trip, leaving Le Domaine in Quebec's De La-Vérendrye Park.
PROVINCE OF QUEBEC
FILM BUREAU PHOTO

DE LA-VÉRENDRYE PARK. Six canoe trips—from two to ten days—are available in the park of about five thousand square miles, with fishing for pike, walleye, and lake trout.

The park covers the headwaters of five great drainage basins—upper Outaouais, the Gatineau, Dumoine, and Coulonge rivers—all Outaouais tributaries—and of Bell, whose waters flow into the Nottaway and James Bay. The park is seamed with rocky ridges. Its mean altitude is some twelve hundred feet above sea level, and its numerous lakes and reservoirs differ greatly in shape and size.

Access routes: from the south, Route 11 (Hull—Maniwaki—Grand-Remous, or Montreal—Mont-Laurier—Grand Remous); and from the north, Route 59 (Malartic—Louvicourt) leads to Route 58, which traverses the entire park.

Waterproof chart (map—one-mile-to-the-inch scale), portages and lengths, rapids, dams, bridges, scenic view stops, points of interest, wilderness camping and group camping spots, $1. Paper charts are free.

Park Office: Le Domaine, Parc de La-Vérendrye, Quebec, Canada.

The canoeist can follow the streams for a long summer cruise and never see a village or dwelling—only picturesque views of distant forested heights, waterfalls and rapids, islands

They've pitched camp before eating at a wilderness camping site in De La-Vérendrye Park, Quebec.
PROVINCE OF QUEBEC FILM BUREAU PHOTO

covered with pine and spruce—and serenity: or, he can rent a cottage or a motel unit designed for comfort. He can also fly in to such a lodge on Lake Parent and be outfitted at a resort.

Reference: Quebec Department of Tourism, Fish and Game Tourism Branch (TB), 930 St. Foy Road, Quebec, Quebec, Canada.

NEW BRUNSWICK

This is the land of memorable, if unpronounceable, rivers. Here run, in crystal clearness, the Miramichi and Restigouche rivers, two of the greatest salmon breeders in the world. On the St. John River trip from Grand Falls to the city of St. John at its mouth, it is possible to take a two-hundred-mile trip with but one portage. Interesting side trips probing tributary rivers and streams are inducements for the wilderness-seeking canoeist.

Reference: Department of Natural Resources, Travel and Tourist Development Branch, 796 Queen St., (P.O. Box 1030), Fredericton, New Brunswick, Canada.

NOVA SCOTIA

In the province of Nova Scotia, forty-three canoe routes beckon the wilderness canoeist, on trails in the counties of Queens, Shelburne, Yarmouth, and Digby. In a dozen places the province is spanned by natural waterways which penetrate the wilds and enable one to travel as the Micmac Indian in bark canoes by water from the alluvial valleys of the Avon, the Annapolis, and the Shubenacodie to the sea-washed southern shore.

Reference: Department of Lands and Forests, P.O. Box 68, Truro, Nova Scotia, Canada, and Nova Scotia Travel Bureau, 5670 Spring Garden Road, Halifax, Nova Scotia, Canada.

CIRCUITS	A	B	C	D	E	F
longueur en milles length miles	15	30	25	43	88	47
durée en jours duration days	1-2	3-5	2-3	4-6	7-10	4-7
PORTAGES						
nombre-number	1	4	4	11	13	14
longeur totale total length miles	⅓	1	¾	2¼	2½	1¾
PARCOURS degree of difficulty						
facile easy	•				•	
moins facile more difficult		•	•			
difficile difficult				•		•

DE LA-VÉRENDRYE PARK
CANOE ROUTES

CANADIAN GOVERNMENT TRAVEL BUREAUS STATESIDE

The Canadian Government Travel Bureau maintains offices in the following cities in the United States: Los Angeles and San Francisco, California; Hartford, Connecticut; Washington, D.C.; Chicago, Illinois; Indianapolis, Indiana; Boston, Massachusetts; Detroit, Michigan; Minneapolis, Minnesota; New York, New York; Rochester, New York; Cincinnati, Ohio; Cleveland, Ohio; Philadelphia, Pennsylvania; Pittsburgh, Pennsylvania; and Seattle, Washington.

U-PADDLE CANOE RENTAL SERVICE

The Hudson's Bay Company has recently established a canoe rental project, based on the

U-Haul car and trailer principle of renting a vehicle at one point and dropping it off at a distant destination. The U-Paddle canoe rental service offers the wilderness canoeist a seventeen-foot aluminum canoe equipped with paddles and a carrying yoke. Food supplies and pertinent advice are given by the post manager (resource person) to help assure a safe and pleasant expedition. The canoes are launched from one post and turned in at another—eliminating the need of backtracking. The trips are routed from posts at various points along famous fur trade water routes. Yellowknife, Waterways, Ile-à-la-Crosse, LaRonge, and Norway House are presently offering U-Paddle service.

Inquiries should be directed to: The Northern Stores-Department, Hudson's Bay Company, Winnipeg 1, Canada.

TAKING PRIVATE PLANES TO CANADA

The Aeronautical Information and Publications Office, Department of Transport, Ottawa, Ontario, Canada, offers free a booklet, *Admission of Aircraft to Canada*. Listed are Canadian sources of information on maps and charts, customs requirements, and airports of entry. Also given are sources of further information, maps showing Flight Information Regions, officially designated "Sparsely Populated Areas" (hinterland), where special rules apply, and areas to avoid. Canada requires that when you fly over hinterland areas you must carry five pounds of concentrated food per person, cooking utensils, matches in a waterproof container, a compass, and other items as part of a survival kit.

Canadian customs regulations present no problems, but it is a good idea, if a choice exists, to select one of the major customs airports for more efficient entry. U.S. Customs requirements for your return can be obtained from the Department of Customs, Washington, D.C. Normally, you must clear Canadian Customs only when entering Canada, U.S. Customs only on your return.

MAPS AND CHARTS OF CANADA

Many a wilderness canoeing trip has run into difficulty for lack of the proper maps or charts. This has been true especially of trips into the hinterland of Canada.

The Canadian government maintains a complete selection of topographical maps and aerial surveys, which are available. The first step in obtaining the map you need is to write for a master index that is divided into seventeen regional indexes. Then select the regional index, by number, that contains the area you are interested in, and order the map. Individual maps measuring 22x29 inches are fifty cents each. The indexes and map lists are free. Order from Map Distribution Office, 615 Booth St., Ottawa 4, Canada.

CANADIAN RAILROADS

The following can give information on proposed canoe routes and country traversed by their respective lines: Canadian National Railways, Montreal, Quebec, Canada; Canadian Pacific Railway, Montreal, Quebec, Canada; Dominion Atlantic Railway, Halifax, Nova Scotia, Canada; Ontario Northland Railway, North Bay, Ontario, Canada.

✂ 17 ✂

Stateside Wilderness

A WILDERNESS experience is possible in nearby waters, for wherever unforeseen conditions develop, civilization can be stripped away and nature challenge the canoeist with all the problems faced by the Indians long before the white man came upon the scene.

There is much uninhabited land along many stateside rivers, and the canoeist can experience the feeling of the wilderness, if but for a matter of hours, should he choose.

For inspirational value, only a few stateside stretches of wilderness are included, with apologies if your favorite retreat isn't mentioned.

To secure information on the wilderness canoeing waters of any state, see Chapter 20 of *Malo's Complete Guide to Canoeing and Canoe-Camping*, Collier Books, paperback, 1970, or write to the Chamber of Commerce of any state, addressed to the capital city, and your query will be referred to the proper office for reply.

ALASKA

Surely, one of the last frontiers, where every river has a wilderness challenge, is found in Alaska. Northwest of Fairbanks are the ideal Yukon and Chatanika rivers, and Birch Creek, and nearby on Eagle Summit the canoeist can witness (around the twenty-first of June) twenty-four hours of "Alaskan Midnight Sun."

Fortymile River from the gold rush days of '96 boasts names like Nugget Gulch, Discovery Creek, and Deadman Rifle, along with mining ghost towns of Franklin, Steele Creek, and Fortymile, which can be seen, moldering away, from the river. Panning for gold can be a lucrative experience.

There are many other routes in Alaska; all the rivers are clear water, except the Yukon and Kenai, which are glacial streams. The streams are rated as to difficulty, access points are designated, as are portages and campsites. There are a minimum of dangerous rapids and long portages. And where else can you fish for grayling, Dolly Varden, red, and silver salmon?

Begin your Alaskan adventure by writing the U.S. Department of the Interior, Bureau of Land Management, Anchorage, Alaska 99501.

CALIFORNIA

The canoeist in the Golden State must look for strips of linear wilderness along the rivers: Colorado, Eel, Klamath, Scott, Smith, Trinity, and Van Duzen. Many coastal streams are canoeable and offer a fisherman's bonanza when the steel-head trout migrate. In the mountain lakes and streams, along with nineteen designated fishing areas, eleven national parks, eleven national forests, and eighteen reclamation lakes, the wilderness canoeist finds some respite from the state's ever burgeoning population.

COLORADO

The fast-moving, narrow, precipitous waters of mountainous Colorado offer, in short stretches, exciting canoeing possibilities. The navigable rivers: Gunnison, Roaring Fork, Arkansas, Yampa, North Platte, and many small streams offer both rugged and serene canoeing with rugged beauty in the mountains, serene loveliness in the pastoral valleys.

The Delta River trip takes the canoeist through a chain of small lakes, each interconnected by a stream, and sheltered by trees, for leisurely travel and fishing.
U.S. DEPARTMENT OF THE INTERIOR: BUREAU OF LAND MANAGEMENT PHOTO

Wilderness canoeing in Illinois.
DEPARTMENT OF CONSERVATION PHOTO

FLORIDA

The Suwannee River rises in Georgia's Okefenokee Swamp and flows through a jungle wilderness (some of it unexplored to this day), gains volume, and widens as it meanders through Florida, where it weaves in exotic beauty toward the Gulf of Mexico.

The Juniper River run is probably the most famous canoe route in the state: from Ocala National Forest, it flows between narrow, twisting banks through unspoiled wilderness. Take-out is at the bridge on State Highway 19. The trip can be made in five hours, but canoeing parties use a week enjoying it and exploring the many interesting side streams.

The Everglades (Flamingo, Florida) is the second largest of the American national parks, and is approximately half water and half land. It is a wildlife sanctuary supreme, with its almost inpenetrable mosaic of lush growth and brackish water. Three canoe trails, recently inaugurated and adequately marked, are designed for those in tune with wild places. The water route weaves through narrow tunnels of mangrove wilderness. The trails are provided with primitive campsites, making them ideal for two-day outings.

Other top rivers in Florida include portions of the St. Johns, Apalachicola, St. Lucie, Myakka, Peace, and others. The wild streams in Florida are mostly in the central and upper part of the state, away from the complex of extensive building development, deep waters, and heavily motorized craft.

IDAHO

The Salmon is Idaho's classic river. Canoe trips are routed from the towns of Salmon and North Fork and traverse the entire state to Riggins, through most primitive country. On this route, you'll be challenging the "River of No Return."

ILLINOIS

The Vermillion River offers to the expert canoeist the best wild stream in the state. To

Paddling white water in Maine.
OLD TOWN CANOE CO. PHOTO

shoot the white water chute known as "Wildcat," better have two paddlers with no gear aboard. To prevent shipping water and swamping, the bow paddler kneels behind the front thwart to bring up the bow. Once through the maelstrom, the crew must quickly maneuver to prevent the canoe from being picked up by the strong upstream current of the back eddy that would take the canoe to the rocks. The Vermillion is not all "Wildcat," however: its banks are forested, and in the spring, the flowering crab, the redbud, and the hawthorn blossoms are spectacular, pine and juniper abound on the bluffs, and wild flowers embroider the timbered slopes along its course. A touch of the wilderness can be experienced on the following rivers: Fox, Sangamon, Kaskaskia, Little Wabash, and the Cache.

IOWA

The Volga River, an out-of-the-way stream, has seen few canoes since Indian days. The moody river (rising rapidly after heavy rains) rushes through a deep valley bounded by high rolling hills and precipitous rock cliffs. A good overnight trip is that from Osborne, on Highway 13, north of Strawberry Point, to Garber on the Turkey River.

The Upper Iowa River is one of Iowa's most beautiful rivers, flowing through one of the deepest valleys in the state. It is fed by numerous springs and tributaries, and maintains a good water level at all seasons. A favorite stretch for the canoeist is that from Kendallville to Decorah. The scenery is superb with limestone cliffs towering in some places four hundred feet above the water. When did you last see a suspension footbridge? The Upper Iowa has one: the county erected it for local children to cross to and from school.

MAINE

The pine tree state probably is the best organized from the standpoint of its canoeing concern — delineating routes, establishing campsites, availability of guides, and cherishing its wilderness. The longest and most difficult route is the St. Johns River 201-mile trip from Northeast Carry to Fort Kent. The most popular trip is the Allagash Lake route from Northeast Carry or Chesuncook Dam and return after ninety miles of tumbling water, heavy timber, portages, and trout fishing. The East Branch of the Penobscot River, racing for 118 miles, takes the canoeist through some typical Maine wilderness experiences. An excellent fishing water is the Grand Lake-Machias River trip (seventy-five miles) from Princeton to Whitneyville. The famed St. Croix is best experienced on the run from Orient at the head of East Grand Lake and cruise into Spednic Lake, picking up the river at Vanceboro, and taking out at Calais ninety-five miles distant. The Bow trip of the Moose River is a rugged one for about fifty miles, which circles back and ends at Attean Lake. The wilderness character of the trip is evidenced by the wild life, deep forests, and some of the largest trout found in a Maine river.

MICHIGAN

The Manistique River, flowing through seventy-five miles of wild, undeveloped country, tests the stamina and resourcefulness of the most ardent paddler. The Presque Isle River, a fast, wild river, races through one hundred miles of rugged country. The "back in the bush" river, skirting the Porcupine Mountains and flowing through some of the most scenic land of the Upper Peninsula, is contained in its lower reaches by vertical cliff shores, and its continuous drop with numerous falls requires portaging. It's the price a canoeist pays to experience this wild portion of Michigan. Sparkling clean water, far from population complexes, are represented by the following rivers, to name a few: Paint, Tahquamenon, Au Sable, Manistee, Pine, and Père Marquette.

ISLE ROYALE NATIONAL PARK, comprising more than eight hundred square miles of land and water, with its timbered ridges, sun-dappled trails, outlying islands, represents an ideal wilderness setting. It is isolated from the mainland by many miles of Lake Superior waters. Forty-five miles of water separate Isle Royale from the nearest Michigan shore, and fifteen miles from the nearest point in Canada. With more than 290 small islands and countless minor rocks surrounding it, Isle Royal is an archipelago of great interest.

The park is distinguished by the great variety of plant and animal life, archeology, fjords, forests, fishing, hiking trails, and its entire realm is devoid of concrete and vehicles.

When did you last see the Indian Pipe, that wax sculpture-like flower that thrives on decayed vegetation? Isle Royale has them, along with the spectacular devil's club, whose natural range belongs to the Pacific Northwest, and thirty-six kinds of orchids growing wild and undisturbed. Berries abound in season, and it's possible to pick blueberries, raspberries, strawberries, and thimbleberries for tasty eating and baking. Covering the island in an interesting example of forest transition are both conifers (cone-bearing trees) and the deciduous (leaf-dropping) trees.

Since 1912, when Lake Superior froze across to Canada and a number of moose ventured over the ice, they have been seen near the lake, along the streams, and on the shores of inland lakes. Smaller animals, such as beaver, muskrat, mink, and weasel, are common, as are also the red squirrel, snowshoe rabbit, red fox, wolf, and coyote. Over two hundred species of birds have been observed on the island, including the rare bald eagle, osprey, and pileated woodpecker.

Fishing licenses are not required on the over thirty inland lakes which contain such game fish as pike, perch, and trout. As boats are unavailable for rental on inland lakes, the canoeist has an advantage.

In prehistoric times, the island was visited

Carrying canoe and packsacks over portage in Minnesota.

PHOTO BY WALTER H. WETTSCHRECK, COURTESY
MINNESOTA CONSERVATION DEPT.

by Indians seeking the native copper along the rocky shores and in the bedrock. They separated the copper from the stone by heating it, then dashing cold water upon it. White men discovered artifacts—arrowheads, knives, cedar shovels, and fragments of pottery—suggesting that these miners were the ancestors of present Algonquian and Siouan tribes. Artifacts of Isle Royale copper have been found as far away as in Aztec country in the Southwest, evidence of the extent of trade carried on by these early people.

HOW TO GET TO THE PARK: Boat service is available from Houghton and Copper Harbor, Michigan, and Grand Portage, Minnesota. Information on schedules can be obtained about May 1, by contacting the Superintendent, Isle Royale National Park, Houghton, Michigan.

MINNESOTA

The gopher state claims more fresh water than any other state in the Union, with 1,900 miles of trout streams, 13,100 miles of inland rivers, and 15,291 lakes. A canoe trail 310 years old, traveled by Radisson and Groseilliers in 1660, is contained in the Shangri-La of canoeing waters—the Boundary Waters Canoe Area—the Superior National Forest of the United States combined with Quetico Provincial Park of Ontario, Canada, discussed in the previous chapter. The combined areas, totaling 400,000 acres of virgin forest, represent the greatest canoe country in the world, the vast wilderness of 14,500 square miles annually drawing 100,000 canoeists from all parts of the United States, Canada, and many foreign countries. The labyrinth of lakes is tied together by a variable meandering of interesting streams and channels. These unique waterways make the Superior-Quetico an unparalleled wilderness facility. Families, church and scout groups, high school and college youths, businessmen, socialites, take off from three main stateside gateways: Grand Marais, Ely, and Crane Lake—all in Minnesota, where excellent outfitting is available to assure a pleasant trip, whether it be a pleasure weekend or a wilderness trip lasting a month.

So extensive are the water trail possibilities that there is no need for backtracking. The lore of the past is everywhere; canoeists of the 1970s can traverse the same water routes, hike over the same portages, and make camp on the same sites as did the Voyageurs of the 1700s.

Minnesota's Big Fork River journeys 173 miles and several hundred years into the past. The route was used by Indians, fur traders, loggers, missionaries, and early settlers, who, too, must have enjoyed its natural wonders: stately pines, massive hardwoods, somber spruce, fragrant balsam, fields of wild rice,

fur-bearing animals, waterfowl, and moose— a rare stateside view these days.

The Little Fork River for 123 miles offers the sighting of moose in the muskeg swamps, deer browsing in the open meads, bear in the woods, beaver, muskrat, and waterfowl along the feeder streams. The fishing is for musky and walleye pike. Thus, a river that offers moose, beaver, and musky qualifies as a wilderness water.

MISSOURI

These days, the canoe is offering the traditional Johnboat a lot of competition along Missouri's famous spring-fed, gravel- and sand-bottomed, cliff-banked, and sand-barred streams. The water runs clean and cool, and the fishing and the scenery are superb in such notable streams as the Big Piney, Eleven

The scenery is superb in Missouri.
RICHLAND MFG. CO. PHOTO

Point, Gasconade, Current, Meramec, Jacks Forks, Elk, Niangua, and Huzzah.

MONTANA

There are many wilderness streams in the state more accessible to the canoe than by foot or any other vehicle: the Madison, Missouri, Yellowstone, Clark Fork of the Columbia, and the Big Hole rivers have a great wilderness potential in this sparsely settled land. The Madison River trips are from Varney Bridge near Cameron to Ennis Lake, and the lower Madison from Gray Cliff Access to the headwaters of the Missouri. From Toston to Townsend on the Missouri River is a recommended two-day trip. Probably Montana's most famous waterway is the Missouri River of Lewis and Clark's epic penetration in search of the Northwest Passage to the Pacific. This portion of the river remains untouched since the two explorers gazed upon the white cliffs, strange rock formations, and teeming wild life.

NEW HAMPSHIRE AND VERMONT

The Connecticut River, historic, venerable, and austere, threading from Canada between New Hampshire and Vermont offers the canoeist, in its four hundred miles, an insight into the past and the beauty of the present. The peacefulness enjoyed by our ancestors seems to rub off onto the modern canoeist who plies the picturesque, wide, and meandering river. The river's short stretches of wilderness are broken up by New Hampshire's majestic pine hills, and Vermont's farm lands, apple orchards, and historic churches.

NEW YORK

The streams in the Adirondacks offer many canoeing experiences, particularly the Fulton Chain Lakes region. The Delaware River between Hancock and Port Jarvis represents an ideal water for canoeists who like to fish in wild places for smallmouth bass and walleyes, brown and rainbow trout.

PENNSYLVANIA

One of the best canoeing rivers in the East is the North Branch of the Susquehanna River, a favorite route being from the New York state line to Tunkhannock. The state provides launching sites in many sectors of the river; at one mile east of Hallstead, two miles north of Oakland, two miles northeast of Sayre, two miles south of Towanda; on Route 6, and one mile south of Tunkhannock. These take-in and take-out access areas provide the canoeist with ample access to the best sections of the North Branch of the Susquehanna.

VIRGINIA

Many streams in the state are seldom canoed because they are difficult to reach, but the canoeist with a little pioneer spirit in his make-up can discover his own solitude. The Rappahannock River is Virginia's contribution to wilderness canoeing. The stretch from Remington to Fredericksburg represents the wildest water highway in the state. The ledges, rapids, white water, and wild country remind the canoeist that he is traveling in the wilderness through which Grant marched his Army of the Potomac during the Civil War.

Paddling below Big Eddy Falls in Wolf River.
WISCONSIN CONSERVATION DEPT. PHOTO

WEST VIRGINIA

Recommended experiences are canoeing the New River in its eighty-mile run from Glen Lyn to Gauley Bridge, and the South Branch of the Potomac for seven miles through a wilderness gorge between Moorefield and Romney.

WISCONSIN

The canoeist could spend an entire summer exploring the Flambeau River complex, long recognized as one of the best white water rivers in the Midwest. Experts relish its challenge. Floating the Flambeau, the canoeist is hemmed in by old-growth pine, hemlock, and hardwoods that have been spared to preserve its wilderness character. A rare sight is the stand of virgin timber, which gives the present-day Voyageur an insight into the type of country Wisconsin's first canoeists paddled along every day.

In early history, the Bois Brule was the gateway leading from Lake Superior to Wisconsin's interior, and eventually to the Mississippi River. Today, it remains a wild river, roaring its way through wooded and rocky

Reaching the wilderness in shorter time with an outboard motor.
EVINRUDE MOTOR DIVISION PHOTO

country. During low water on the boulder-strewn river, the canoeist must call upon his poling technique to negotiate the ruffled water.

The St. Croix River, indicated as one of America's "Scenic Rivers," runs deep and fast through uninhabited forested land, and at times between towering banks. Along its course from Solon Springs are stretches of rapids with spuming white foam, quietness for a while, then the river roars again, alternating these conditions in a stimulating change of pace as the miles are traversed.

OTHER STATES

The canoeist must discover his own wilderness challenges in the rivers of the following states:

ARKANSAS: White, Buffalo, and the Little Missouri rivers.

GEORGIA: Flint, St. Marys, Satilla, Suwannee rivers.

INDIANA: Tippecanoe, Kankakee, St. Joseph, Wabash rivers.

Canoeing in Kansas.
TRAILCRAFT CANOE
CO. PHOTO

KANSAS: Arkansas, Big Blue, Cimarron, Neosha, Marais des Cygnes rivers.

KENTUCKY: Green, Salt, Licking, Red, Nolin, Elkhorn rivers.

MISSISSIPPI: Pearl, Chunky, Bowie, Bogue, Chitto rivers.

NEW JERSEY: Delaware, Maurice, Passaic, Raritan rivers.

OHIO: Little and Great Miami, Mohican, Maumee, Sandusky rivers.

OREGON: Lower Rogue, Little, Upper Deschutes, Umpqua rivers.

TENNESSEE: Wilbur, Watauga, Daniel Boone, Norris, Chilhowee rivers.

UTAH: Portions of the rugged Green and Colorado white water rivers.

WASHINGTON: Columbia, Snake, Spokane rivers, and coastal streams.

WYOMING: Portions of the Green and Platte rivers.

OUTWARD BOUND

The Outward Bound approach to motivating young people (sixteen to twenty-three years of age) was developed by Dr. Kurt Hahn, founder and headmaster of the famed Gordonstoun School in Scotland, in an effort to devise a means for steeling young men against needless defeatism—physical or mental. Aware of the increasing aimlessness of youth, their lack of involvement and failure to mature into whole adults, Dr. Hahn feels that a boy must learn for himself how much he is capable of, physically, emotionally, and spiritually. If a boy can be made to stretch to his full stature, he will not shrink again to a lesser self. But one cannot tell a boy, "You are capable of more"; a set of circumstances must be devised through which he can learn for himself.

The first Outward Bound School was organized in Britain (1941), and now there are twenty-three throughout the world. Since 1962, five have been established in the United States: Colorado, Minnesota, Maine, Oregon, and North Carolina.

The programs of the schools are oriented to their sea, mountain, and water wilderness environments. All schools include intensive training in search and rescue, fire-fighting, first-aid, drown-proofing, and lifesaving techniques.

The Ely, Minnesota, school specializes in wilderness canoeing; after preliminary training there, the students go to the north shore of Lake Superior in preparation for an eleven-day expedition into the wilderness, where the method of instruction is to confront the students, day and night, with a series of anxiety-, even panic-creating, situations unlike anything they have ever before faced.

Some time after the training phase, each student enters the wilderness alone, generally on an island, carrying a knife, six matches, some salt, material for catching game, a first-aid kit, and some basic equipment for protection against extreme weather conditions. The student will be taught either to live off the land, or to fast for the duration of the solo, which is often the most difficult as well as the most creative part of the program because of its emotional impact.

It means something different to each person—rest, loneliness, fear, boredom, peace, contemplation, new direction. David S. Potter, Union College, summarized his experience: "Solo, blitzing mosquitoes the first night, crayfish and one ugly sculpin for lunch, loons calling as the setting sun was severed by low western clouds, the long pale arch of aurora borealis, blueberries and water for another meal, warm ashes slowly igniting birch bark peelings to start again a flickering flame, and finally a plump walleye pulled onto the rocks as a noisy woodpecker called in the crisp, pale light of the third dawn."

All students learn the fine points of white water canoeing in preparation for the long expedition.
MINNESOTA OUTWARD BOUND SCHOOL PHOTO

The tuition to Outward Bound is four hundred dollars, but half of the young men are admitted on scholarship to effect a greater diversity in the make-up of each group. As Peter O. Willauer, director of the Maine school puts it, "You get a boy from an Ivy League college crawling down the side of an eighty-five-foot cliff. His life may depend on the Puerto Rican kid from the slums of New York who is holding the safety rope at the top. The Ivy Leaguer doesn't ask if the Puerto Rican is in the Social Register—his only concern is that the boy at the top has ability and will power to hold onto the safety rope if it is needed."

The Outward Bound movement is growing to include young women and businessmen. It has been used as a part of management training programs by some of Britain's largest industries, and today many United States businessmen are being exposed to its philosophies. Corporation presidents feel that their executives fail because they lack self-confidence, desire, and determination to succeed despite obstacles, competition, and momentary setbacks. They gladly pay the tuition to Outward Bound to instill traits of maturity, character, confidence, the will to succeed, and an addiction to excellence.

The address: Outward Bound, Inc., Andover, Mass. 01810.

AMERICAN YOUTH HOSTELS, INC.

Canoeists with kindred wilderness ambitions can be found in the membership of the AYH, 20 West 17th St., New York, N.Y. 10011, whose purpose includes . . . to gain a greater understanding of the world and its people, through outdoor activities, educational and recreational travel and related programs. Since 1934 canoeing has remained a popular activity with AYHers. Local chapter canoe trip chairmen annually plan a trip program, and more experienced canoeists are served with a trip or two into the wilderness. By all means, get in touch with a local group if one is nearby.

Other Organizations

There are always adventure-bent members in other organizations, many of which include canoeing in their programs. A crew can be filled-out by contacting interested members in local chapters of many national organizations: Audubon Society, Sierra and Alpine Clubs, Scout Explorers, Izaak Walton League, and bird, hiking, and camping groups.

WILD AND SCENIC RIVER SYSTEM

Stateside canoeists can be heartened by the recently established (October 2, 1968) National Wild and Scenic River System to keep some of our remaining wild rivers unobstructed, preserving them in their natural free-flowing state, free of the threat of dams, pollution, and other assault.

The bill, originally proposed by Senator Frank Church of Idaho, extends 300 feet on either side, to keep the rivers primitive and undeveloped, avoiding commercialism that would destroy the scenic values along the riverbanks.

The original committee, after considering many, established the initial system to include segments of: the Salmon and the Clearwater, including its tributaries—the Lochsa and the Selway in Idaho; portions of the Rogue River in Oregon; the Rio Grande in New Mexico; Eleven Point in Missouri; and the Cacapon and Shenandoah Rivers in West Virginia.

Some of the National Scenic Rivers areas include: the St. Croix in Wisconsin and Minnesota, the Illinois River in Oregon, and the Namekagon in Wisconsin.

The bill further provides for Federal-State studies to determine the further inclusion of the following: Buffalo, Tennessee; Green, Wyoming; Hudson, New York; Missouri, Montana; Niobrora, Nebraska; Skagit, Washington; Susquehanna, New York and Pennsylvania; Wolf, Wisconsin; Suwannee, Georgia and Florida; Little Miami and Little Beaver, Ohio; and Pine Creek and Clarion in Pennsylvania.

Senator Church hopes that eventually the effect will extend to nearly every state, so that we will have a Wild River system that is nationwide in scope.

Many conservationists believe that the Wild River bill lacks teeth, that dams can be constructed by Act of Congress, and that the unspoiled rivers be placed under National Park jurisdiction as was done with the Current River in Missouri: however, canoeists are thankful for this tangible evidence of concern for our waterways.

✵ 18 ✵

Home
Again

THE canoeist comes from the wilderness with a welter of experiences that bring a new dimension to life and strengthen some resolves: one, to evaluate his trip to reap the maximum benefits of good planning in the future; and, two, to advocate the proper husbandry of our natural resources of pure air and clean water.

WRAPPING UP YOUR WILDERNESS TRIP

In order to avoid any repetition of discomfort resulting from poor planning, a good canoeist makes a complete evaluation of each just-completed trip—the sooner the better—a good time being on the trip home, although undoubtedly, all along the way he has been jotting self-directions in his notebook, such as: Get a better compass, a longer painter.

Add more hard candy to the rations; more trinkets and tobacco for the Indians. Take along more naphtha soap to grease the bottoms of pots; more scouring pads, skeeter dope; an additional pair of canvas gloves for cooking. Repair pack straps, a rip in the tent, etc.

Evaluation is the Making of a Bushman

The detailed thoroughness with which a wilderness canoeist evaluates the trip is of immense help when planning for future ones. These questions are by no means comprehensive: each canoeist has additional elements and areas to be considered.

1. Was the community equipment and gear adequate?
   A. What replacements are needed?
   B. What repairs needed?
   C. Items to be added?

D. Eliminate on the next trip?

2. Was each crew member's clothing and gear adequate?

A. What additions?

B. What changes?

3. First-aid kit adequate?

A. Items to be added;

B. Replacements of material used.

4. List of all items lost: when and where replace them?

5. Was the food ample?

A. The menus savory?

B. The cooking kit satisfactory?

6. Was the season right for:

A. Weather?

B. Water level?

C. Absence or minimum presence of insects?

7. What about the locale? The extent of the trip?

8. The outfitter's service and supplier? Satisfactory?

9. Accuracy and satisfaction of services of the contact person?

Answers to these questions may be jotted down on your original planning lists and filed for the next trip's planning sessions.

This veteran canoeist recalls over-burdening himself on his first trip, swinging to the opposite extreme on his second; then becoming a stickler for a more valid (rational) list of equipment—measuring, weighing, and changing his list until an efficient one was evolved.

Regardless of the number of canoe trips you take, don't despair over deficiencies: veteran outdoorsmen always complain about "The stuff I forgot!"

Homecoming

At the conclusion of a wilderness trip, there's joy in breaking camp the last time: and as there have been some sacrifices in the food department, the canoeist (as soldiers returning from overseas duty) gorges on nostalgic fare—hamburgers, hot dogs, chocolate malts, ice cream, crisp salads, and perhaps a cold beer—the while eagerly planning for the subsequent season's trip. Through it all run the brightly colored threads of a developing sensitivity, from firsthand experience, to the needs of the lesser wilderness brothers, the urgency of measures needed for the proper husbandry of our natural resources.

The canoeist lives and loves deeply the back roads, and they become a part of him, for in concord with the universe, each realizes that he is no less than the sky and the stars, the trees and the hills: yet, neither is he above the lichen and the moss, the milkweed and the mushroom. In this biotic enterprise, each is one with all fellow creatures, an absolute unity, which at its basic level constitutes only truth—what Emerson called the "oversoul," a philosophy of inquiry into the nature of life and of man, the understanding of each individual that each creature and thing is intimately related with the other.

Man's component dimension in the universe is neither above nor below other components: mountains, oceans, and forests; laurels, plankton, and field mice; lichens, algae, or chlorophyll. All, as man, are a part of the family pattern, and he in the total scheme is no special son, having no right to dominate or to endanger any of his brothers: all are committed to silent codes which, when abrogated, find retribution to be lightning quick.

The wilderness canoe trails, as with mountain magnitudes, forest fastnesses, and the seas' purity, are vulnerable to this one brother, especially in his direction to manipulate, control, and drastically alter his environment, to exploit the earth's riches, to decimate wild life, rather than to live in harmony with the laws that govern the intricate "web of life." Yet, that brother is constantly reminded of his minor role, and that his achievements have done little more than to scratch the surface of the limitless works of God.

A quiet time alone in the wilderness is the fount for contemplation of these truths that are eternally valid—listening to your own song, poem, or prayer rendered to the rhythm of your heartbeat, the pulsations of the trees, or the cadence of the waves. In the evening, lie on a rock ramp warm from the retained heat of the sun's beneficence, under an inverted bowl of stars and aurora's colors, and an awareness of what is real, what is artificial, emerges like a bright sunrise to bathe you in a sense of holiness.

Common things become divine when man learns to respect the world around him, meets it on its own terms, understanding that nothing lives unto itself, that the Fates are neither harsh, stern, nor unfair, and vows that as one brother, he will not lacerate the protective soil skin, gash the trees, desecrate the external environment upon which he is today so precariously and feebly perched, and will strive to become attuned to the totality of life, to maintain the integrity of the grand plan.

CONSERVATION IS MANDATORY

This is becoming the era of conservation, for man has discovered that he is the No. 1 endangered species. Evidences of self-imposed possible doom are everywhere: pesticide-infested surroundings, sewage-choked waters, poisonous gases, garbage and litter dumps, and paved-over landscapes; an estimated 140 million tons of dust, fumes, smoke, carbon dioxide, soot, sulphur dioxide, and other wastes spewed into the air each year;

rivers so polluted with oil that they are fire hazards; fish and game unsafe for eating because of DDT and mercury concentrations in their flesh; all the major river systems polluted, the Great Lakes dead or dying, etc.

The canoeist, well versed in environmental realities, takes his place, first in local efforts to curb pollution, to safeguard the waterways, to halt needless draining of the wetlands and the headlong building of dams, then allies himself with organizations, battle-scarred, but triumphant, in many conservation campaigns: The Johnny Horizon pledge to keep the land clean and free of litter, respect and treat the land as "my own," obey state game and fish laws, and be careful with fire; the duck hunters who led the campaign to establish the Migratory Bird treaty with Canada; fishermen who fostered stream-improvement programs; the Izaak Walton League, which has taken its place (since 1920) as one of the surging conservation forces of all time; the country's college campuses participating in an "Environmental teach-in"; and dedicated men and women, active and forceful, in such organizations as Sierra and Alpine Clubs, Wilderness Association, Audubon Society, Conservation Commissions, Open Lands Project, and Clean Streams Committee.

Organizations, as every unattached citizen, must feed observations into an environment computer for the interpretation of citizen, sportsman, or organization leader who can develop the political muscle necessary to move programs in the proper direction—perhaps eventually leading to an "Environment Pentagon," where the best minds in ecology, biology, anthropology, botany, chemistry, and related sciences will comprise a board dealing with the salvation of our precious resources, including mankind.

❦ ❦ ❦

INDEX

❦ ❦ ❦

Index

173